Best Easy Day Hikes
Bend and Central Oregon

Help Us Keep This Guide Up to Date

Every effort has been made by the author and editors to make this guide as accurate and useful as possible. However, many things can change after a guide is published—trails are rerouted, regulations change, facilities come under new management, etc.

We would love to hear from you concerning your experiences with this guide and how you feel it could be improved and kept up to date. While we may not be able to respond to all comments and suggestions, we'll take them to heart and we'll also make certain to share them with the author. Please send your comments and suggestions to the following address:

> The Globe Pequot Press
> Reader Response/Editorial Department
> P.O. Box 480
> Guilford, CT 06437

Or you may e-mail us at:

> editorial@GlobePequot.com

Thanks for your input, and happy trails!

Best Easy Day Hikes Series

Best Easy Day Hikes Bend and Central Oregon

Second Edition

Lizann Dunegan

FALCONGUIDES®

GUILFORD, CONNECTICUT
HELENA, MONTANA
AN IMPRINT OF THE GLOBE PEQUOT PRESS

FALCONGUIDES®

Maps created by XNR Productions, Inc. © 2009 Morris Book Publishing, LLC

ISSN 1547-7282
ISBN: 978-0-7627-5103-7

Printed in the United States of America

10 9 8 7 6 5 4 3 2 1

Contents

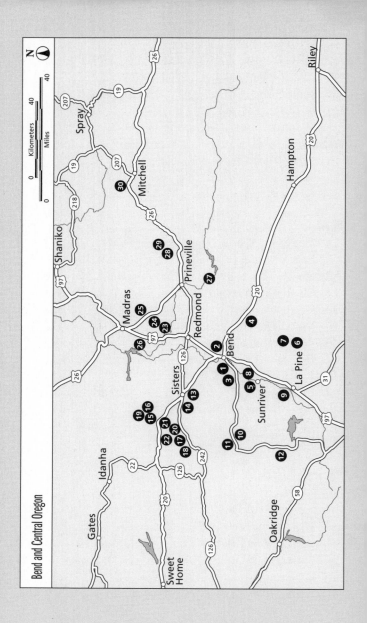

Bend and Central Oregon

Acknowledgments

Thanks to Ken Skeen for his editorial advice; to Bear, my canine hiking companion; and to Josh Rosenberg for editing the manuscript.

Introduction

This small pocket guide contains thirty easy day hikes ranging from 0.25 mile to 8.6 miles that allow you to explore Bend and surrounding natural areas in Central Oregon. A high-desert ecosystem of sagebrush, juniper, and ponderosa pine characterizes the dry central part of this state, where volcanic activity and erosion have formed amazing gorges and unique rock formations.

Coursing through all of this is the mighty Deschutes River, beginning high in the Cascade Mountains and traveling north to south through the heart of Bend, Central Oregon's largest city.

Many consider Bend the gateway to the High Cascade Lakes Region and Deschutes National Forest. It serves as the geographic and popular center to this area of the state. Many hikes off the Cascade Lakes Highway promise wonderful mountain and lake views, such as the Green Lakes Trail, the Ray Atkeson Memorial Trail, and Osprey Point. If you're looking for trails in town, check out the Pilot Butte State Park, Shevlin Park, First Street Rapids Park—Deschutes River Trail, and Deschutes River Trail—Benham Falls to Slough Meadow routes.

Afterward, consider visiting the Newberry National Volcanic Monument, which can be easily accessed from the city of Bend (it's southeast of Bend off U.S. Highway 97). Home to Newberry Caldera, a 500-square-mile crater that houses Paulina and East Lakes, this national monument has a rich geologic history, evident in its hot springs, lava flows, and cinder cones. The 0.7-mile Big Obsidian Flow Trail takes you on a fascinating tour of Oregon's youngest lava flow. To see the national monument from a different perspective, try the Paulina Lake Loop, which circles scenic Paulina Lake.

Located northwest of Bend, the small Western town of Sisters is a major access point to both the Mount Washington and Mount Jefferson Wilderness Areas—serious volcano country. Two trails not to be missed here are Hand Lake and Little Belknap Crater. Hand Lake Trail takes you along the shores of scenic Hand Lake and offers stunning views of Mount Washington. Little Belknap Crater Trail takes you across the moonlike landscape of an ancient lava flow. From the summit of the crater you can enjoy sweeping views of the snow-topped Three Sisters Mountains, Mount Washington, and the surrounding lava flows and craters that make up the Mount Washington Wilderness. For a pristine river hike, take a tour on the West Metolius River Trail and admire the lush, spring-fed river ecosystem. If you enjoy waterfalls, check out the Squaw Creek Falls hike.

Located 5 miles northeast of Redmond, Smith Rock State Park is also located in the center of this open, high-desert country. It features spectacular pinnacles, columns, and cathedral-like cliffs that rise more than 400 feet above a mammoth gorge carved by the Crooked River. Tour this unusual landscape on a 3.2-mile out-and-back trail, located about 8 miles northeast of Redmond off US 97. If you are looking for solitude, explore the Gray Butte and Rimrock Springs Natural Area hikes. Both are located within a thirty-minute drive of Redmond in the Crooked River National Grasslands and feature high-desert scenery.

Around Prineville, try the Chimney Rock hike, which promises solitude and nice views of the Crooked River canyon and distant Central Cascade peaks. A less frequently visited but no less stunning area is the Mill Creek Wilderness, located about 20 miles northeast of Prineville off U.S. Highway 26. Twin Pillars Trail takes you through this wilderness, characterized by open, parklike stands of ponderosa pine, grand fir, and Douglas fir forests. Another destination not to be missed is the Painted Hills Unit of the John Day Fossil Beds National Monument. Several short hikes in this area feature close-up looks at the area's fossil beds and beautifully colored hills.

Weather

Unlike the Willamette Valley to the west, the central part of the state is much sunnier and dryer. The average annual rainfall in this part of the state is 12 inches, and blue skies are the norm. Summer temperatures range from the mid-70s to low 90s; winter temperatures can range from the mid-20s to mid-50s. Be prepared for a substantial amount of snow in the high mountain areas above 4,000 feet and periodic snow showers at lower elevations. Hikes at elevations above 4,000 feet may not be accessible until late June into early July.

Preparing for Your Hike

Planning your hiking adventure begins with letting a friend or relative know your trip itinerary so that they can call for help if you don't return at your scheduled time. Your next task is to make sure you are outfitted to experience the risks and rewards of the trail. This section highlights clothing and gear that can help you get the most out of your day hike.

Clothing

Clothing is your armor against Mother Nature's little surprises. Clothing that can be worn in layers is a good strategy for dealing with the often unpredictable Central Oregon weather. In spring, fall, and winter, the first layer you'll want to wear is a wicking layer of long underwear that keeps perspiration away from your skin. Long underwear made from synthetic fibers is an excellent choice. These fabrics wick moisture away from the skin and draw it to the next layer of clothing, where it then evaporates. Avoid long underwear made of cotton; it is slow to dry and keeps moisture next to your skin.

Your second layer should be an insulating layer. In addition to keeping you warm, this layer needs to "breathe" so that you stay dry while hiking. One fabric that provides insulation and dries quickly is fleece; a zip-up jacket made of this material is highly recommended.

The last line of layering defense is the shell layer—some type of waterproof, windproof, breathable jacket that'll fit over all your other layers. It should have a large hood that fits over a hat. You'll also need a good pair of rain pants made from a similar waterproof, breathable fabric.

Now that you've learned the basics of layering, don't forget to protect your hands and face. In cold, windy, or rainy weather, you'll need a hat made of wool or fleece. Insulated, waterproof gloves will keep your hands warm and toasty. They'll allow you to remove your outer gloves for close work without exposing the skin.

During the warm summer months, you'll want to wear a wide-brimmed hat, sunglasses, and sunscreen. If you're hiking in spring or summer on a trail next to a lake, creek, or river, be sure to carry mosquito repellent in your pack.

Shoes and Socks

Lightweight hiking boots or trail running shoes are an excellent choice for day hiking. If you'll be hiking in wet weather often, boots or shoes with a Gore-tex liner will help keep your feet dry.

Socks are also another important consideration. Steer clear of cotton socks in favor of socks made of wool or a synthetic blend. These socks provide better cushioning, wick moisture away from your feet, and help prevent blisters.

It's a good idea to bring an extra pair of sandals or an old pair of tennis shoes along if you plan on wading in creeks or swimming in rivers.

Once you've purchased your footwear, be sure to break them in before you hit the trail. New footwear is often stiff and needs to be stretched and molded to your foot for optimum comfort.

Backpacks

A day pack to carry basic trail essentials will help make your day hike more enjoyable. A day pack should have some of the following characteristics: a padded hip belt that's at least 2 inches wide (avoid packs with only a small piece of nylon webbing for a hip belt); a chest strap (which helps stabilize the pack against your body); external pockets to carry water and other items that you want easy access to; an internal pocket to hold keys, a knife, a wallet, and other miscellaneous items; an external lashing system to hold a jacket or windbreaker; and a pocket for carrying a hydration system (a water bladder with an attachable drinking hose). Some hikers like to use a fanny pack to store just a camera, food, a compass, a map, and other trail essentials. Many fanny packs have pockets for two water bottles and a padded hip belt.

Day Hiking Checklist

- day pack
- water and water bottles/water hydration system
- food; high-energy snacks
- first-aid kit
- GPS unit or compass and map
- sunscreen and sunglasses
- matches in waterproof container and fire starter
- insulating top and bottom layers (fleece, wool, etc.)
- rain gear
- winter hat and gloves
- wide-brimmed sun hat, sunscreen, and sunglasses
- insect repellent
- backpacker's trowel, toilet paper, and resealable plastic bags
- camera/film
- cell phone
- guidebook
- watch

Trail Regulations/Restrictions

Trails in this guide are located in city parks, state parks, national scenic areas, national forests, and Bureau of Land Management (BLM) lands. Trails located in city parks in this guide do not require special permits or charge use fees.

Trailhead fees at some national forest and national scenic area trailheads require a Northwest Forest Pass. You can buy a day pass for $5 or an annual pass for $30. For participating national forests and locations for purchasing a Northwest Forest Pass, call (800) 270–7504 or go online to www.fs.fed.us/r6/passespermits/. A majority of Oregon's state parks require a $3 day-use permit, or you can purchase a $25 annual state park permit. You can purchase passes at self-pay machines located at state park trailheads and visitor centers. To purchase an annual state park pass, call (800) 551–6949 (credit card orders only) or visit www.oregon.gov/oprd/parks/index.shtml.

Trail Contacts

Hikes 1 and 3: Bend Metro Park & Recreation District, 200 Northwest Pacific Park Lane, Bend, OR 97701; (541) 389–7275; www.bendparksandrec.org.

Hikes 2, 23, and 26: Oregon Parks and Recreation Department State Parks, 725 Summer Street NE, Suite C, Salem, OR 97301; (800) 551–6949; www.oregon.gov/oprd/parks/index.shtml.

Hike 4: Bureau of Land Management, Prineville District Office, 3050 Northeast Third Street, Prineville, OR 97754; (541) 416–6700; www.blm.gov/or/districts/prineville/index.php.

Hikes 5–12: Deschutes National Forest, 1001 SW Emkay Drive, Bend, OR 97702; (541) 383–5300; www.fs.fed.us/r6/centraloregon.

Hikes 13–22: Deschutes National Forest, Sisters Ranger District, P.O. Box 249, Sisters, OR 97759; (541) 549–7700; www.fs.fed.us/r6/centraloregon.

Hikes 24 and 25: Crooked River National Grassland, 813 Southwest Highway 97, Madras, OR 97741; (541) 475–9272; www.fs.fed.us/r6/centraloregon.

Hikes 27, 28, and 29: Ochoco National Forest, 3160 Northeast Third Street, Prineville, OR 97754; (541) 416–6500; www.fs.fed.us/r6/centraloregon.

Hike 30: John Day Fossil Beds National Monument, 32651 Highway 19, Kimberly, OR 97848; (541) 987–2333; www.nps.gov/joda.

Zero Impact

The trails in Central Oregon are quite popular and sometimes can take a beating. We, as trail users and advocates, must be especially vigilant to make sure our passing leaves no lasting mark.

These trails can accommodate plenty of human travel if everyone treats them with respect. Just a few thoughtless, badly mannered, or uninformed visitors can ruin the trails for everyone who follows. The book *Leave No Trace* is a valuable resource for learning more about these principles.

Three Falcon Zero-Impact Principles:
- Leave with everything you brought.
- Leave no sign of your visit.
- Leave the landscape as you found it.

Most of us know better than to litter. It is unsightly, polluting, and potentially dangerous to wildlife. Be sure you leave nothing behind, regardless of how small it is. Pack out all your own trash, including biodegradable items like orange peels, which might be sought out by area critters. Also consider picking up any trash that others have left behind.

Follow the main trail. Avoid cutting switchbacks and walking on vegetation beside the trail. Select durable surfaces, such as rocks, logs, or sandy areas, for resting spots.

Don't pick up souvenirs, such as rocks, shells, feathers, driftwood, or wildflowers. Removing these items will take away from the next hiker's experience.

Avoid making loud noises that may disturb others. Remember, sound travels easily along ridges and through canyons.

Finally, abide by the golden rule of backcountry travel: If you pack it in, pack it out! Thousands of persons coming after you will be thankful for your courtesy.

Map Legend

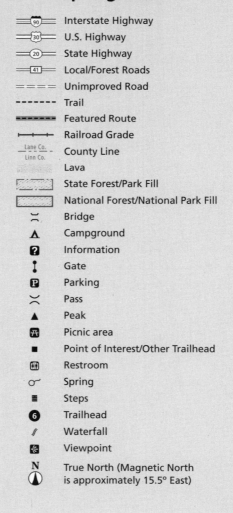

═══⟨90⟩═══	Interstate Highway
═══⟨30⟩═══	U.S. Highway
═══⟨20⟩═══	State Highway
═══⟨41⟩═══	Local/Forest Roads
═ ═ ═ ═	Unimproved Road
- - - - - - -	Trail
▬▬▬▬▬	Featured Route
├──┼──┤	Railroad Grade
Lane Co.‾ ‾ ‾ ‾ Linn Co.	County Line
	Lava
	State Forest/Park Fill
	National Forest/National Park Fill
⏝	Bridge
▲	Campground
❷	Information
⦙	Gate
🅿	Parking
⏜	Pass
▲	Peak
⏏	Picnic area
■	Point of Interest/Other Trailhead
⊞	Restroom
⟲	Spring
≡	Steps
❻	Trailhead
∥	Waterfall
⮜	Viewpoint
N ⬥	True North (Magnetic North is approximately 15.5° East)

Bend

1 First Street Rapids Park–Deschutes River Trail

This easy route, located in downtown Bend, rambles along a scenic section of the Deschutes River. The trail begins at First Street Rapids Park and heads north along the river's edge. After about a mile you'll parallel a golf course as the trail winds through a mix of juniper, sage, and yellow-barked ponderosa pine trees. The last half of the trail winds high on the canyon rim and affords stunning views of Mount Washington and Black Butte to the northwest and the Deschutes River far below.

Distance: 6.0 miles out and back.

Approximate hiking time: 2½ to 4 hours.

Elevation gain: 120 feet.

Trail surface: Dirt path, wood chip trail.

Best season: Open year-round. Snow may be present during the winter months.

Other trail users: Joggers and mountain bikers.

Canine compatibility: Leashed dogs permitted.

Fees and permits: No fees or permits required.

Schedule: Open dawn to 10 p.m.

Maps: Maptech CD: Coos Bay/ Eugene/Bend, OR.

USGS map: Bend, OR.

Finding the trailhead: From U.S. Highway 97 (Business) in Bend, turn right onto Division Street. Go 0.7 mile and turn right onto Revere Avenue. Continue 0.1 mile and turn left onto Wall Street. Proceed 0.3 mile and turn right onto Portland Avenue. Go 0.3 mile and turn right onto First Street. Continue 0.3 mile to where the street dead-

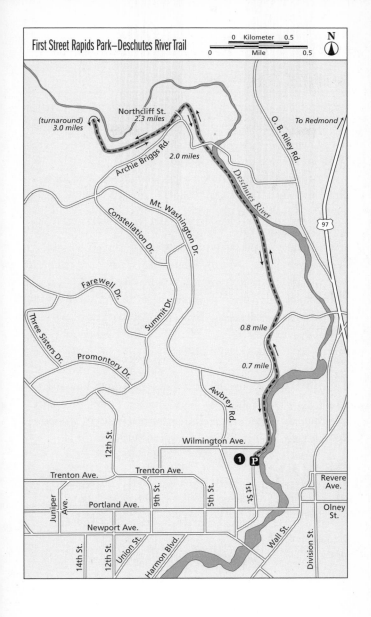

First Street Rapids Park–Deschutes River Trail

0   Kilometer   0.5

0   Mile   0.5

N

(turnaround)
3.0 miles

Northcliff St.
2.3 miles

Archie Briggs Rd.

2.0 miles

O. B. Riley Rd.

To Redmond

Deschutes River

97

Constellation Dr.

Mt. Washington Dr.

FareWell Dr.

Three Sisters Dr.

Summit Dr.

Promontory Dr.

0.8 mile

0.7 mile

Awbrey Rd.

12th St.

Wilmington Ave.

Trenton Ave.

Trenton Ave.

9th St.

5th St.

1st St.

1

P

Revere Ave.

Juniper Ave.

Portland Ave.

Olney St.

Newport Ave.

14th St.

12th St.

Union St.

Harmon Blvd.

Wall St.

Division St.

ends at First Street Rapids Park. *DeLorme: Oregon Atlas & Gazetteer:* Page 51 D6.

The Hike

First Street Rapids Park is one of the many parks in Bend that line the banks of the Deschutes River. The majority of the route is on a wide, wood chip trail that parallels the Deschutes River through downtown Bend.

First Street Rapids Park is a popular put-in spot for kayakers, and most likely you'll see paddlers playing in rapids at the park. From the trailhead the wide wood chip trail heads north along the river. Watch for small groups of ducks, blue herons, and Canada geese feeding along the riverbank. At 0.8 mile you'll cross Mount Washington Drive and continue on a wood chip trail as it continues north. At this point the trail parallels the smooth greens of the River's Edge Golf Course and then enters a forest corridor that passes through several residential areas. This is one of twenty-four golf courses located in Central Oregon.

Over the next 2 miles you'll cross two more paved roads as the path winds through an area of expensive homes high above the river. From this high vantage point, the snow-capped peaks of Mount Washington, Black Butte, and other Central Cascade peaks dominate the skyline to the west.

Miles and Directions

0.0   From First Street Rapids Park, begin hiking north on the wood chip trail that parallels the scenic Deschutes River.

0.7   Turn left on the wood chip trail (don't go right toward the golf course). The trail intersects paved Mount Washington Drive. Turn right and follow the wood chip trail downhill as it parallels Mount Washington Drive. (Look for the small DESCHUTES

RIVER TRAIL signs marking the trail.)

0.8   Turn left and cross Mount Washington Drive. Pick up the wood chip trail on the other side. (The trail parallels a paved path for a short distance but then turns back to wood chip only.)

2.0   Cross Archie Briggs Road and continue on the wood chip trail on the other side.

2.3   The trail crosses unmarked Northcliff Street in a residential area and then hugs the ridgeline high above the Deschutes River. (FYI: From this section of the trail you'll have grand views of Mount Washington, Black Butte, and other Central Cascade peaks.)

3.0   Arrive at the route's turnaround point. Retrace the route back to your starting point.

6.0   Arrive back at the trailhead at First Street Rapids Park.

2 Pilot Butte

This hike, located in downtown Bend, climbs 480 feet to the summit of Pilot Butte—a prominent cinder cone situated on the east side of Bend. From the summit you'll have spectacular views of Mount Bachelor, the Three Sisters, Broken Top, and Black Butte, as well as many other Cascade peaks. You also have the option of hiking an additional 3.4 miles out and back on the Larkspur Trail, which travels to the Bend Senior Center and Larkspur Park.

Distance: 1.7 miles out and back.

Approximate hiking time: 45 minutes to 1½ hours.

Elevation gain: 480 feet.

Trail surface: Paved path and dirt path.

Best season: Open year-round. Snow may be present during the winter months.

Other trail users: Joggers.

Canine compatibility: Leashed dogs permitted.

Fees and permits: No fees or permits required.

Schedule: Open dawn to 10 p.m.

Maps: Maptech CD: Coos Bay/ Eugene/Bend, OR.

USGS map: Pilot Butte, OR.

Finding the trailhead: From Northeast Third Street/U.S. Highway 97 (Business) in Bend, turn east onto Greenwood Avenue/U.S. Highway 20. Continue 1.4 miles and turn left onto Northeast Azure Drive at the second PILOT BUTTE TRAILHEAD sign. Follow signs for another 0.3 miles to a large parking area and trailhead. *DeLorme: Oregon Atlas & Gazetteer:* Page 51 D6.

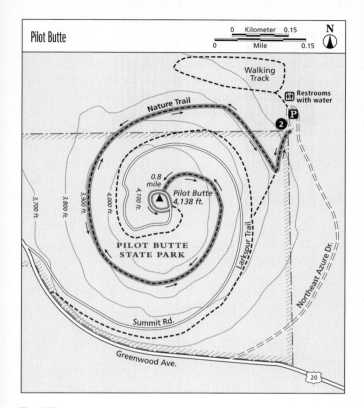

Pilot Butte

Walking Track

Restrooms with water

Nature Trail

0.8 mile

Pilot Butte 4,138 ft.

3,700 ft.
3,800 ft.
3,900 ft.
4,000 ft.
4,100 ft.

PILOT BUTTE STATE PARK

Larkspur Trail

Northeast Azure Dr.

Summit Rd.

Greenwood Ave.

20

The Hike

This scenic route climbs 480 feet to the summit of Pilot Butte in downtown Bend. Pilot Butte is an extinct cinder cone and a well-known Central Oregon landmark. The first European settlers in this area called the formation "Red Butte" due to its reddish-colored soil.

The route starts at the base of the butte, where you'll find restrooms with water, picnic tables, a walking track, and interpretive signs. You also have the option of walking on the 3.4-mile out-and-back Larkspur Trail that you can access from the same trailhead. You'll follow the well-graded trail as it winds at a fairly steep pace around the butte. Rest benches and interpretive signs are interspersed along the trail if you want to take a break. From the summit you'll enjoy a 360-degree view of downtown Bend and the surrounding high-desert country and Central Cascade peaks. After walking around the summit circle, you'll retrace the same route back to the parking area.

Miles and Directions

0.0 Start hiking on the paved path adjacent to the parking area.

0.1 Turn right on the signed dirt nature trail. Continue uphill on the smooth singletrack trail that climbs to the 4,138-foot summit of Pilot Butte. (**Option:** You can continue straight on the paved Larkspur Trail that continues 1.7 miles to the Bend Senior Center and Larkspur Park.)

0.8 Turn right onto the paved summit road. Walk around the paved summit circle and take time to stop and soak in the gorgeous view of Mount Bachelor, Broken Top, the Three Sisters, Mount Washington, and other Central Cascade peaks.

0.9 Turn right and retrace the same route back to your starting point.

1.7 Arrive back at the trailhead.

3 Shevlin Park Loop

This fun hike is a local favorite and is only minutes from downtown Bend. The route winds through ponderosa pine and Douglas fir forest along the banks of picturesque Tumalo Creek in Shevlin Park.

Distance: 4.9-mile loop.

Approximate hiking time: 2 to 3 hours.

Elevation gain: 250 feet.

Trail surface: Dirt path, double-track dirt road.

Best season: Open year round. Snow may be present during the winter months.

Other trail users: Joggers and mountain bikers.

Canine compatibility: Leashed dogs permitted.

Fees and permits: No fees or permits required.

Schedule: Open dawn to 10 p.m.

Maps: Maptech CD: Coos Bay/ Eugene/Bend, OR.

USGS map: Bend, OR.

Finding the trailhead: From Northeast Third Street/U.S. Highway 97 (Business) in Bend, turn west onto Greenwood Avenue. Continue 0.4 mile. Continue straight on Northwest Newport Avenue (this road becomes Shevlin Park Road after a few miles) and proceed 3.8 miles. Turn left at the signed Shevlin Park entrance and park in the paved parking area by the wood trail sign. *DeLorme: Oregon Atlas & Gazetteer:* Page 51 C5.

The Hike

The city of Bend is host to 2,375 acres of developed parks and open spaces and over 48 miles of trails. This route explores 652-acre Shevlin Park, which was donated by the Shevlin-Hixon Company to the city of Bend in 1920. The

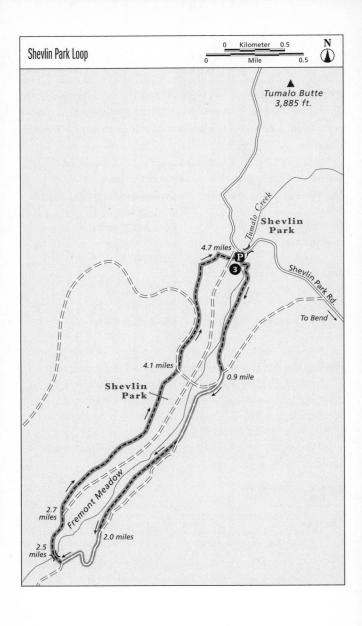

Shevlin Park Loop

0 Kilometer 0.5
0 Mile 0.5

N

▲ Tumalo Butte
3,885 ft.

Tumalo Creek

Shevlin Park

4.7 miles

P
3

Shevlin Park Rd.

To Bend

4.1 miles

0.9 mile

Shevlin Park

Fremont Meadow

2.7 miles

2.5 miles

2.0 miles

park was named for the company's president, Thomas H. Shevlin. At one time Shevlin-Hixon operated one of the largest lumber mills in the country. Its first mill in Bend opened in 1916 and began processing what seemed to be an endless supply of trees. By 1950 the tree supply began to dwindle and Shevlin-Hixon sold out to its rival, Brooks-Scanlon.

This route is very convenient to downtown Bend and is very popular. You'll begin by hiking through a stand of shimmering aspen trees and then crossing rambling Tumalo Creek. After crossing the creek you'll walk up a short hill on some switchbacks to the top of the ridge. The route hugs the ridgeline above the creek through an old-growth ponderosa pine forest blanketed with leafy green manzanita. The stately ponderosa pine tree forms parklike stands and can be recognized by its yellowish bark and large cylindrical cones. The trees can grow to heights of more than 120 feet and live to be 400 to 500 years old. Periodically the park is subjected to prescribed burns to keep the forest healthy by eliminating dead brush and promoting new growth.

From the ridgeline the trail descends back to the creek. You'll cross a picturesque wood bridge and finish the loop on a combination of singletrack and doubletrack back to your starting point. Be cautious of mountain bikers, who also enjoy this fun loop.

Miles and Directions

0.0   From the paved parking area, go around a metal gate. Start walking on the singletrack trail, which starts on the left side of a large wood trail sign.

0.1   Turn left and follow the singletrack trail for about 100 yards until you reach a wood bridge over Tumalo Creek. Cross the bridge, turn right, and follow the singletrack trail about 25 yards upstream. The trail then curves sharply to the left and switchbacks steeply uphill.

0.2 Turn right at the T intersection.

0.3 Turn right at the trail fork and continue hiking through a clear-cut area on a high ridge above the creek.

0.8 Turn left, ignoring the spur trail that heads downhill to the creek.

0.9 Turn right onto a doubletrack road.

1.2 Turn right onto a singletrack trail.

1.9 Turn left and continue on the singletrack trail along the ridge. Ignore the singletrack trail that heads downhill to the right.

2.0 Turn right onto a doubletrack road. The route takes you downhill toward the creek. Then you'll cross over a drainage pipe and head uphill.

2.1 Turn right onto a doubletrack road. Go about 25 yards and arrive at a T intersection. Turn left onto a singletrack trail.

2.5 Cross a narrow wood bridge over Tumalo Creek. After crossing the bridge continue on the singletrack trail as it heads downstream.

2.7 Arrive at a somewhat confusing five-way intersection. Go left onto an unsigned singletrack trail that heads slightly uphill.

4.0 Turn right onto a singletrack trail.

4.1 Cross a doubletrack road and continue on the singletrack trail.

4.7 Turn left onto the paved park entrance road.

4.9 Arrive back at the trailhead.

4 Dry River Gorge

This hike explores an ancient river gorge in the heart of Central Oregon's high desert. The route passes through an old-growth juniper forest and affords many opportunities to see ravens, hawks, and other wildlife.

Distance: 6 miles out and back.

Approximate hiking time: 2 to 3 hours.

Elevation gain: 300 feet.

Trail surface: Dirt path.

Best season: March through May and September through October. Avoid this hike during July and August, when temperatures can exceed 90 degrees.

Other trail users: Equestrians.

Canine compatibility: Dogs permitted.

Fees and permits: No fees or permits required.

Schedule: Open year-round. Snow may be present during the winter months.

Maps: Maptech CD: Coos Bay/ Eugene/Bend, OR.

USGS maps: Horse Ridge, OR; Millican, OR.

Finding the trailhead: From Bend head east on U.S. Highway 20 to Milepost 17. From Milepost 17 continue 0.5 mile and turn left onto an unsigned doubletrack dirt road. Cross a cattleguard and continue straight (right) on a doubletrack road that goes between two large gravel piles. Go 0.8 mile on this doubletrack road (you'll have to weave around some rocks in the road) to a primitive campsite on the right. Turn right into the campsite and park. If you have a high-clearance vehicle, you have the option of continuing 0.3 mile farther on this road. The remaining 0.3 mile is not recommended for passenger vehicles due to several large rocks in the road. *DeLorme: Oregon Atlas & Gazetteer:* Page 76 A1.

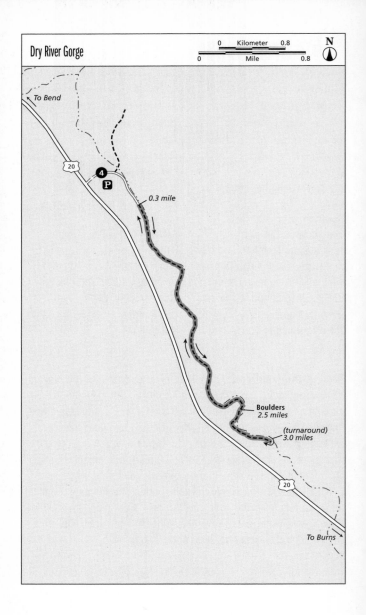

Dry River Gorge

0   Kilometer   0.8

0   Mile   0.8

N

To Bend

20

4
P

0.3 mile

Boulders
2.5 miles

(turnaround)
3.0 miles

20

To Burns

The Hike

This route follows the course of a prehistoric river through a magnificent rocky gorge. The river that once flowed here drained a large ice lake, which formed east of the gorge when lava flows created a natural dam. During episodes of high rainfall, the lake would overflow over a low pass located at the eastern edge of Horse Ridge. This strong, coursing flow of water cut through the porous lava, creating this magnificent river gorge. The river flowed north and eventually drained into the Crooked River. Groups of Native Americans camped around this ancient lake, and pictographs have been found on the rocks in the gorge.

This out-and-back hike takes you deep into the canyon, which is filled with old-growth western juniper trees. These hardy trees blanket the Central Oregon region and make up the second largest juniper forest in the world. Western junipers grow well in the hot sun and can thrive on less than 8 inches of rain per year. The small, fragrant, bluish berries of the juniper are a favorite food of small mammals and birds. Other plants that thrive in this desert landscape are fragrant-smelling sagebrush, rabbitbrush, and bitterbrush. During the spring months delicate wildflowers add splashes of color to the trail.

As you walk on the trail you'll be amazed by the bright lime-green and orange lichens that cover the canyon walls. These high rimrock canyon walls are also a perfect place for raptors and ravens to nest. At 0.9 mile and 2.2 miles, you'll pass old-growth ponderosa pines that have managed to survive in this very dry canyon. At 2.5 miles the trail seems to abruptly come to an end. You have the option of turning around here, or, if you are feeling adventurous and don't mind scrambling over rocks, you can continue on the trail. After you scramble over several large boulders on the right, you'll see the continuation of the rocky trail that has been carved into the right side of the canyon. You'll follow this rocky trail for 0.1 mile and then descend to the canyon floor. From here the sandy trail continues in a southeast direction. Continue for another 0.4 mile to the trail's end at the opposite end of the canyon. As you are hiking in the canyon, be on the lookout for rattlesnakes that sometimes make an appearance.

Miles and Directions

0.0   Start by walking south on the main doubletrack road. Turn right at a road junction; you'll continue walking on a doubletrack road for 0.3 mile.

0.3   The wide doubletrack road ends next to a primitive campsite. Continue hiking on the singletrack trail that heads into the canyon.

0.9   Arrive at a large ponderosa pine tree on the left side of the trail.

2.2   Pass another large ponderosa pine tree.

2.5   Arrive at a large boulder field, where the trail abruptly seems to end. You have the option of turning around here or continuing on the trail by scrambling over a series of boulders on your right and continuing on a rocky path. The path continues for 0.1 mile and then descends back down to the canyon floor.

2.6   The rocky section ends. Continue your journey up the canyon on a smooth sandy trail.

3.0   Arrive at the end of the trail and your turnaround point at the end of the canyon.

6.0   Arrive back at the trailhead.

5 Deschutes River Trail–Benham Falls to Slough Meadow

This route follows the southern segment of the Deschutes River Trail. It takes you through a magnificent old-growth ponderosa pine forest along the banks of the moody Deschutes River. Highlights include a spectacular viewpoint of Benham Falls, grand views of South Sister and Broken Top, and opportunities to see ospreys and other wildlife.

Distance: 4.6 miles out and back (with a shuttle option).

Approximate hiking time: 3 hours.

Elevation gain: 100 feet.

Trail surface: Dirt path.

Best season: Open year-round. The driest months are May through October. Snow may be present during the winter months.

Other trail users: Mountain bikers, joggers.

Canine compatibility: Leashed dogs permitted.

Fees and permits: A $5 Northwest Forest Pass is required. You can purchase a pass online at www.naturenorthwest.org or by calling (800) 270-7504.

Schedule: Open all hours.

Maps: Maptech CD: Coos Bay/Eugene/Bend, OR.

USGS map: Benham Falls, OR.

Finding the trailhead: From the intersection of Northwest Franklin and U.S. Highway 97 (Business) in Bend, travel 11.2 miles south on US 97 to the LAVA LANDS VISITOR CENTER sign. Turn right (west) onto the entrance road and then take an immediate left onto Forest Road 9702, where a sign indicates DESCHUTES RIVER 4/BENHAM FALLS 4. Continue 4 miles to a gravel parking area at Benham Falls Day Use Picnic Area.

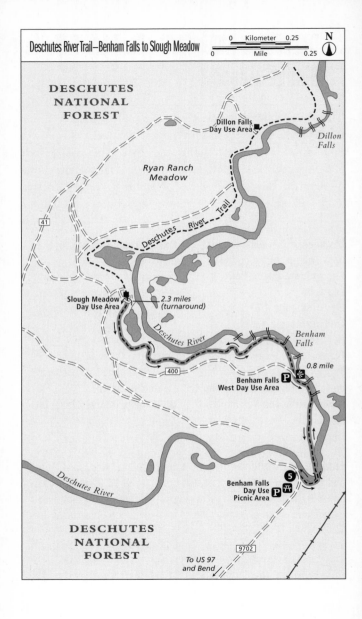

0   Kilometer   0.25

0   Mile   0.25

N

DESCHUTES NATIONAL FOREST

Dillon Falls Day Use Area

Dillon Falls

Ryan Ranch Meadow

41

Deschutes River Trail

Slough Meadow Day Use Area

2.3 miles (turnaround)

Deschutes River

Benham Falls

0.8 mile

400

Benham Falls West Day Use Area

P

5

Benham Falls Day Use Picnic Area

P

Deschutes River

DESCHUTES NATIONAL FOREST

9702

To US 97 and Bend

Shuttle directions to Meadow Day Use Area: Head 6.2 miles west of Bend on the Cascade Lakes Highway (Highway 46) and turn left onto gravel Forest Road 100 at the MEADOW PICNIC AREA sign. Continue 1.4 miles to the parking area and trailhead. *DeLorme: Oregon Atlas & Gazetteer:* Page 45 A5.

The Hike

This route starts at the picturesque Benham Falls Day Use Picnic Area, which is set among towering old-growth ponderosa pines. The day-use area has picnic tables, fire rings, and restrooms. You'll begin the hike by walking on a forested path along the shores of the Deschutes River. The river is very quiet and wide along this section due to a man-made logjam above the wood bridge across the river. This logjam was built in the 1920s to help protect bridge pilings from debris floating down the river. Plants and grass have grown on top of the logs, creating an "almost" natural dam on the river. At 0.1 mile you'll cross the river over a long wood bridge. For the next 0.5 mile you'll walk on a wide multiuse path that is popular with mountain bikers. At 0.7 mile you'll turn off the multiuse path onto a hiking trail that follows the contours of the river. As you approach Benham Falls, the character of the river changes from slow and meandering to fast and furious as the river channel narrows. At 0.8 mile you'll arrive at a spectacular viewpoint of Benham Falls, where the river roars over jagged lava through a narrow canyon. From here the route continues along the shores of the river. You'll have views of a magnificent lava flow on the opposite side of the river and spectacular views of South Sister and Broken Top. Ospreys feed and nest along this section of the river. Also known as fish hawks, they feed on the large stocks of trout present in the river.

You can identify ospreys by their predominantly white undersides and black markings on the top of their wings. Their heads are white, with a distinctive black band across their eyes and cheeks. Look for their nests, which are usually located in the tops of dead trees. At 2.3 miles you'll arrive at your turnaround point—Slough Meadow Day Use Area.

If you are interested in a longer hike (or completing this hike as a shuttle), you can continue on the Deschutes River Trail for another 6.2 miles to Meadow Day Use Area.

Miles and Directions

0.0   Start hiking on the trail signed DESCHUTES RIVER TRAIL NO. 2.1, which begins at the river's edge opposite the picnic area. Another sign indicates BENHAM FALLS ½, DILLON FALLS 3½, LAVA ISLAND FALLS 7, MEADOW DAY USE 8½.

0.1   Cross a long wood bridge over the Deschutes River.

0.6   Veer right on the hiking trail, indicated by a hiker symbol.

0.7   The hiking trail intersects the wide biking trail. Turn right and continue on the narrower hiking trail. Proceed about 200 yards to a T intersection. Turn right and descend to a viewpoint of Benham Falls. (If you go left at this junction, you'll arrive at the Benham Falls West Day Use Area, which has restrooms.)

0.8   Arrive at a scenic viewpoint of Benham Falls. After enjoying the view, turn around and head uphill on the same trail to a trail junction. Turn right where a sign indicates SLOUGH MEADOW 1.5 MILES.

0.9   Arrive at an interpretive sign on the right that describes the geology of this area. At this point you'll also have spectacular views of Broken Top and South Sister.

1.1   Turn right and continue on the hiking trail, indicated by a hiker symbol.

| **2.3** | Arrive at the Slough Meadow Day Use Area (your turnaround point). Retrace the same route back to the trailhead. (**Shuttle option:** You can continue 6.2 miles to the Meadow Day Use Area. See "Finding the Trailhead" for directions to this trailhead.) |
| **4.6** | Arrive back at the Benham Falls Day Use Picnic Area. |

6 Big Obsidian Flow

The Big Obsidian Flow Trail is an easy and convenient way to check out Oregon's youngest lava flow. Located in Newberry National Volcanic Monument, this fascinating path crosses the lava flow and highlights the volcanic history of the area. Interpretive signs along the way explain how Native Americans visited the area to collect obsidian for making jewelry and tools.

Distance: 0.7-mile loop.

Approximate hiking time: 30 minutes to 1 hour.

Elevation gain: 300 feet.

Trail surface: Paved path, stairs.

Best season: Late June through October.

Other trail users: None.

Canine compatibility: Leashed dogs permitted.

Fees and permits: A $5 Northwest Forest Pass is required. You can purchase a pass at the entrance booth to the monument or online at www.naturenorthwest.org or by calling (800) 270-7504.

Schedule: Open dawn to dusk.

Maps: Maptech CD: Coos Bay/Eugene/Bend, OR.

USGS map: East Lake, OR.

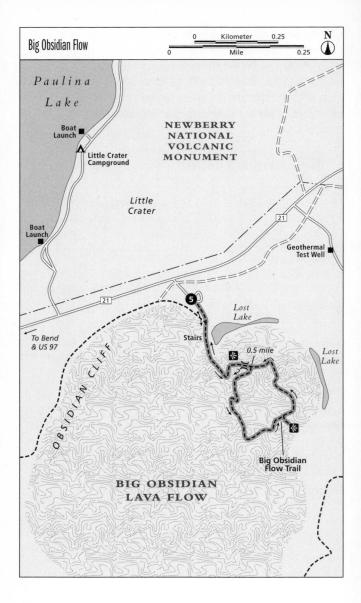

Big Obsidian Flow

0   Kilometer   0.25
0   Mile   0.25

N

Paulina Lake

Boat Launch

Little Crater Campground

NEWBERRY NATIONAL VOLCANIC MONUMENT

Little Crater

Boat Launch

21

Geothermal Test Well

5

Lost Lake

Stairs

0.5 mile

Lost Lake

21

To Bend & US 97

OBSIDIAN CLIFF

Big Obsidian Flow Trail

BIG OBSIDIAN LAVA FLOW

Finding the trailhead: From the intersection of Greenwood Avenue and U.S. Highway 97 (Business) in Bend, travel south on US 97 for 23 miles to a sign for Newberry National Volcanic Monument and Paulina and East Lakes. Turn left on Paulina Lake Road (Forest Road 21) and drive 15.4 miles to the Big Obsidian Trailhead parking area on the right side of the road. *DeLorme: Oregon Atlas & Gazetteer:* Page 45 C7.

The Hike

One of the main attractions at the 55,000-acre Newberry National Volcanic Monument is the Big Obsidian Flow Trail, which provides a fascinating tour of Oregon's youngest lava flow. The trail, which begins as a flat, paved path, offers panoramic views of the flow and includes interpretive signs intended to make understanding the landscape easy. The lava rock is very sharp, so be sure to wear sturdy shoes.

After a short distance the path ascends a steep set of metal stairs and, at the top, arrives at the flow itself—a vast spread of gray pumice interspersed with shiny glasslike boulders of obsidian.

Just past the stairs, the trail comes to a T intersection. From here you can go right or left to begin a 0.3-mile loop. The loop offers outstanding views of 7,984-foot Paulina Peak and Paulina and East Lakes, located at the center of 500-square-mile Newberry Crater.

The 1,300-year-old flow, which covers 1.1 square miles and has an average thickness of 150 feet, began as extremely hot magma (up to 1,600 degrees Fahrenheit) trapped by the earth's crust 2 to 4 miles underground. The magma eventually found weak points in the earth's surface, and a violent eruption ensued. Later, as the eruption slowed, the sticky magma began oozing out of the earth and crawling over the landscape.

One of the more interesting features of the present-day rough and jumbled flow is the glasslike obsidian found on its surface. Due to the way obsidian is formed (through rapid cooling of lava), it is very hard and extremely sharp. These properties were highly valued by Native Americans, who called the rock Isukws (pronounced "eshookwsh"). They made arrowheads, knives, jewelry, ornaments, sculptures, ceremonial objects, and tools out of the obsidian to trade with other tribes for fish, shells, and roots. Artifacts dating back 10,000 years have been found in the monument and surrounding areas. You can read about these relics of the past as you walk the trail.

Miles and Directions

0.0   Start hiking on the paved path by the parking area.

0.1   Ascend a set of metal stairs to the lava flow.

0.2   Turn right to begin the loop portion of the trail.

0.5   Turn right (this is the end of the loop).

0.7   Arrive back at the parking area.

7 Paulina Lake Loop

This hike takes you on a tour of Paulina Lake in the Newberry National Volcanic Monument.

Distance: 7.5-mile loop.
Approximate hiking time: 3 to 4 hours.
Elevation gain: 230 feet.
Trail surface: Gravel path, dirt path, paved road.
Best season: Late June through October.
Other trail users: None.
Canine compatibility: Leashed dogs permitted.

Fees and permits: A $5 Northwest Forest Pass is required. You can purchase a pass at the entrance booth to the monument or online at www.naturenorth west.org or by calling (800) 270-7504.
Schedule: Open dawn to dusk.
Maps: Maptech CD: Coos Bay/ Eugene/Bend, OR.
USGS map: Paulina Peak, OR.

Finding the trailhead: From the intersection of Northwest Franklin and U.S. Highway 97 (Business) in Bend, travel 23 miles south on US 97. Turn left (east) onto Forest Road 21 (Paulina Lake Road). After 11.6 miles you'll pass the entrance booth to the national monument on your left. Continue 1.6 miles past the entrance booth to the Paulina Lakeshore Trailhead on the left. *DeLorme: Oregon Atlas & Gazetteer*: Page 45 C6.

The Hike

At first glance, Central Oregon may be characterized by its wide-open spaces, sagebrush- and juniper-scattered plateaus, rounded buttes, forested ridges, and snowcapped mountains. But not far off the main highways are some of the most unique and dramatic features in the world—

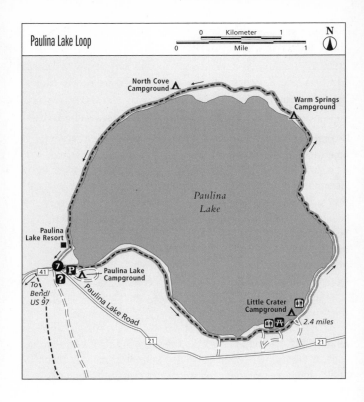

the dramatic remains of volcanic activity that, geologically speaking, occurred fairly recently.

One of the most stunning of these geological features can be seen at 50,000-acre Newberry National Volcanic Monument, located southeast of Bend off US 97. This national preserve was established in 1990 as the volcanic centerpiece of the Central Oregon region. At the heart of this preserve is the 500-square-mile Newberry Caldera crater, which cradles two pristine alpine lakes—Paulina and East.

Paulina Lake (250 feet deep) and East Lake (180 feet deep) were a single, very large lake until lava flows split them apart approximately 6,200 years ago. Today these two lakes are designated as a wildlife refuge, supporting bald eagles, ducks, geese, ospreys, and tundra swans. Mammals roaming the shores and surrounding peaks and valleys include badgers, black bears, deer, elk, and pine martens. Both lakes are popular fishing spots for trout and other fish.

Newberry Volcano is located along a group of faults called the Northwest Rift Zone and is one of the largest shield volcanoes in the United States. Shield volcanoes are formed mainly by fluid lava flows pouring from a central vent to form a broad, gently sloping, dome-shaped cone. The volcano's most recent activity occurred 1,300 years ago, when it deposited more than 170 million cubic yards of obsidian and pumice into what is now called Big Obsidian Flow, located just east of Paulina Lake Lodge.

This fun hike circles Paulina Lake. The route takes you past prime swimming beaches, piles of shiny black obsidian, and stellar views of 7,984-foot Paulina Peak. Be prepared for cool weather—and bring plenty of mosquito repellent.

Miles and Directions

0.0   From the paved parking area, start around the lake in a counterclockwise direction on the signed Paulina Lakeshore Trail. The trail starts out as a gravel path lined with stones.

0.1   Hike across a paved boat ramp and then continue walking on the signed trail. Not far past this junction, a sign indicates LITTLE CRATER CAMPGROUND 2.5 MILES.

1.5   The trail seems to fade out. Continue following the lakeshore.

1.7   The trail is evident again and becomes a long grassy track next to an inviting sandy beach.

2.2   Arrive at a paved boat ramp that has a restroom and picnic tables. After crossing the paved boat ramp, you'll arrive at a sign that states PAULINA LAKESHORE LOOP TRAIL/TRAIL FOLLOWS ROAD. From this point follow the paved road as it parallels the lakeshore.

2.4   Arrive at the entrance to Little Crater Campground. Continue on the paved road through the campground as it follows the lakeshore.

2.5   Pass a restroom and a water faucet. Follow the road through the campground until it ends. Turn right into a gravel trailhead parking lot and pick up the Paulina Lakeshore Trail. There are two trails at this parking area. Take the trail going left. (FYI: The trail goes around a rocky point with cool lava outcroppings and fantastic views of Paulina Peak. Watch your footing over the next mile—it is rocky and filled with tree roots.)

4.0   Turn right at the trail sign.

4.5   The trail begins climbing a high ridge above the lake for the next 0.5 mile.

5.0   Begin descending the ridge on a series of long sweeping switchbacks back to the lakeshore.

6.9   Pass several vacation cabins on your right. The trail becomes faint here; keep following the lakeshore.

7.0   Turn right onto a gravel road next to the Paulina Lake Resort general store.

7.1   The road becomes pavement.

7.2   Turn left onto the unsigned dirt singletrack trail.

7.3   Turn left onto a paved road and then cross a concrete bridge over Paulina Creek. Immediately after crossing the bridge, turn left and go down a set of stone steps to pick up the unsigned dirt trail.

7.5   Arrive back at the trailhead.

8 Lava Lands Visitor Center Trails

This route combines two trails: the Trail of the Molten Land and the Trail of the Whispering Pines. The first trail takes you on a journey through an amazing lava flow to a viewpoint with spectacular views of the Central Cascade Mountains. The second trail winds through a second-growth ponderosa forest and has interpretive signs explaining the plants, animals, and history of this area.

Distance: 1.1 miles
Approximate hiking time: 30 minutes to 1 hour.
Elevation gain: 295 feet.
Trail surface: Paved path.
Best season: May through October.
Other trail users: None
Canine compatibility: Leashed dogs permitted.

Fees and permits: A $5 Northwest Forest Pass is required. You can purchase a pass at the entrance booth online at www .naturenorthwest.org, or by calling (800) 270-7504.
Schedule: 9:00 a.m. to 5:00 p.m.
Maps: Maptech CD: Coos Bay/ Eugene/Bend, OR.
USGS map: Lava Butte, OR.

Finding the trailhead: From the intersection of Northwest Franklin and U.S. Highway 97 (Business) in Bend, travel 11.2 miles south on US 97 to a LAVA LANDS VISITOR CENTER sign. Turn right (west) and park in the main parking area. *DeLorme: Oregon Atlas & Gazetteer*: Page 45 A5.

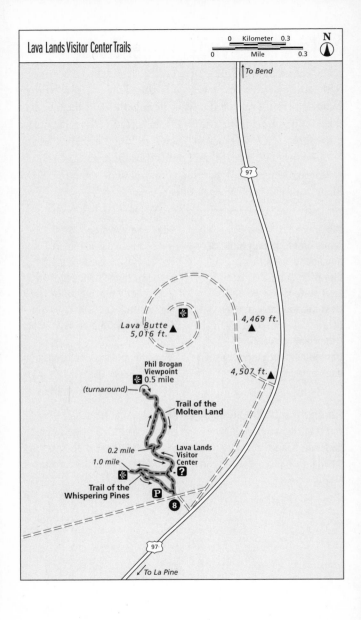

Lava Lands Visitor Center Trails

0   Kilometer   0.3

0   Mile   0.3

N

To Bend

97

Lava Butte
5,016 ft.

4,469 ft.

4,507 ft.

Phil Brogan
Viewpoint
0.5 mile

(turnaround)

Trail of the
Molten Land

0.2 mile

Lava Lands
Visitor
Center

1.0 mile

?

Trail of the
Whispering Pines

P

8

97

To La Pine

The Hike

This short hike takes you on a tour of the moonlike landscape of a spectacular lava flow—the result of an eruption of Lava Butte that occurred between 6,000 and 7,000 years ago. When Lava Butte erupted, the lava flowed in three main channels covering 10 square miles and blocking the Deschutes River in five different locations.

This route begins adjacent to the Lava Lands Visitor Center (open 9:00 a.m. to 5:00 p.m. daily mid-May through mid-September), which is filled with exhibits on the area's geology, animals, and plants. A small selection of maps and books is also available. You'll follow the Trail of the Molten Land as it winds through the lava flow. Interpretive signs help identify important features about the lava flow, including surface tubes and lava channels. After 0.5 mile you'll arrive at the Phil Brogan Viewpoint. From this high vantage point you'll have far-reaching views of the immense lava flow and the Central Cascade Mountains. From here you'll complete the short loop and then continue walking on the Trail of the Whispering Pines. This short interpretive trail weaves through a second-growth forest of ponderosa and lodgepole pines. Interpretive signs describe some of the native plants that grow here including snowbrush, manzanita, and squaw currant. Native Americans used these plants in a variety of ways. The bark and roots of the snowbrush plant were used as an astringent, manzanita seeds were ground into flour, and parts of the squaw currant were used to cure stomach ailments.

Miles and Directions

0.0 From the main parking area start walking on a paved path toward the visitor center. (You'll reach a trail junction before you reach the visitor center.) Turn left on the paved path. Continue about 50 feet to another trail junction. Turn right. (Note: The Trail of the Whispering Pines goes left at this junction.) At the next trail junction, continue straight on the signed Trail of the Molten Land.

0.2 Turn left at the trail junction.

0.3 Turn left toward the signed Phil Brogan Viewpoint.

0.5 Arrive at the Phil Brogan Viewpoint. Take a break on the wood benches and soak in the view of the Central Cascade Mountains and a magnificent lava flow. Walk down the viewpoint trail to the Trail of the Molten Land Trail and turn left.

0.7 The loop portion of the trail ends. Continue straight.

0.9 Turn right at the trail junction toward the signed Trail of the Whispering Pines. Continue 25 yards, and turn right to continue on the paved Trail of the Whispering Pines.

1.0 You have the option of turning right to a small viewpoint.

1.1 The Trail of the Whispering Pines ends at the parking area and your starting point.

⑨ Fall River

This beautiful trail follows the course of the crystal-clear, spring-fed Fall River. This uncrowded route takes you through immense groves of ponderosa pine trees and offers many scenic viewpoints of the river where you may see Canada geese, ospreys, and mallard ducks.

Distance: 6.4 miles out and back.

Approximate hiking time: 2½ to 3½ hours.

Elevation gain: 100 feet.

Trail surface: Dirt path, double-track road.

Best season: April through November.

Other trail users: Mountain bikers.

Canine compatibility: Dogs permitted.

Fees and permits: No fees or permits required.

Schedule: Open all hours.

Maps: Maptech CD: Coos Bay/Eugene/Bend, OR.

USGS map: Pistol Butte, OR.

Finding the trailhead: From the intersection of Greenwood Avenue and U.S. Highway 97 (Business) in Bend, travel 16.7 miles south on US 97. Turn right (west) onto Vandevert Road at the VANDEVERT ROAD/FALL RIVER sign. Continue for 1 mile to the junction with South Century Drive. Turn left and go 1 mile to the junction with Cascade Lakes Highway (Forest Road 42). Go right and continue 10.4 miles (you'll pass Fall River Campground on the left after 9.7 miles) to an unsigned gravel circular parking area on the left side of the road. A green Forest Service building is also located adjacent to the parking area. *DeLorme: Oregon Atlas & Gazetteer:* Page 44 B4.

The Hike

Located in the Deschutes National Forest southwest of Bend, Fall River is a beautiful spring-fed river that is

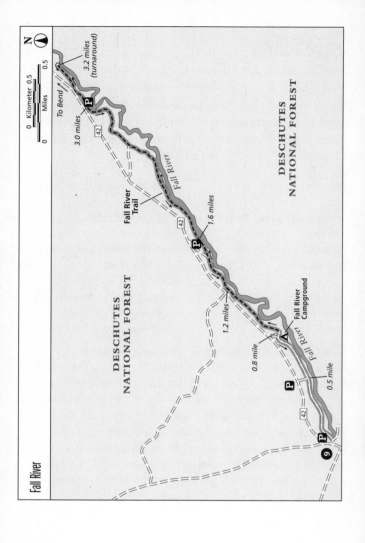

Fall River

N

0 Kilometer 0.5

0 Miles 0.5

To Bend

3.2 miles (turnaround)

3.0 miles

Fall River Trail

Fall River

42

1.6 miles

DESCHUTES NATIONAL FOREST

1.2 miles

0.8 mile

Fall River Campground

Fall River

0.5 mile

42

9

DESCHUTES NATIONAL FOREST

stocked with brown, brook, and rainbow trout. The source of the river is situated about 2 miles northwest of Pringle Falls on the Deschutes River. From this location the river meanders northeast for 8 miles until it joins the Deschutes River about 6 miles below Pringle Falls.

This route parallels the course of the river for 3.2 miles. The tour takes you through a forest corridor of stately ponderosa pine trees. These yellow-barked giants are prized for their clear, even grain, which is used for door and window frames. This hardy tree is fire resistant and survives drought better than any other Northwest tree. The root system is deep and extensively branched, and the tree can survive on only 8 to 12 inches of rain per year. These amazing trees can live to be 400 to 500 years of age and grow to be more than 120 feet tall and 5 feet in diameter.

After 0.7 mile you'll arrive at quiet Fall River Campground. This Forest Service campground has ten tent sites with picnic tables, fire grills, and vault toilets. You'll hike through the campground for 0.1 mile and then continue on the singletrack trail next to Campsite #8. From here the forest deepens, with thick stands of lodgepole pines. These trees are also drought and fire resistant and have the ability to live in poor soils. They grow very slowly, and it may take a century for a tree to reach a height of 60 feet. Native Americans used the long, thin trunks of these trees as supporting poles for their tepee lodges.

As the trail approaches the river's edge, watch for Canada geese and ducks feeding in the river. Also be on the lookout for ospreys perched in dead tree snags along the river's edge. After 1.2 miles you'll walk on a doubletrack road for 0.4 mile and then turn back onto a singletrack trail until the trail's end and your turnaround point at 3.2 miles.

Miles and Directions

0.0 Look to your left and begin hiking on the doubletrack road that begins adjacent to a wood pole fence. Go 75 yards and then veer left onto a smaller doubletrack road. This road soon becomes a wide singletrack trail that takes you through a corridor of large ponderosa pines.

0.5 Arrive at a sign (facing the other way) that states END OF TRAIL/PARKING ON ROAD 42. Ignore the sign and continue heading east as the trail parallels Fall River.

0.6 Veer to the right at the brown hiker sign. (FYI: Just past this junction you'll pass a picturesque wood bridge that spans Fall Creek.)

0.7 Arrive at Fall River Campground Day Use Area. (Restrooms are available on your left.) Turn onto the gravel campground loop road and continue through the campground.

0.8 Veer right on the unsigned singletrack Fall River Trail that begins just to the left of Campsite #8 and takes you through a thick lodgepole pine forest right near the river's edge.

1.2 The trail intersects a red-cinder road. Turn right onto the cinder road.

1.5 Turn right onto an unsigned doubletrack road.

1.6 Turn right onto an unsigned singletrack trail just before the doubletrack road meets a red-cinder road.

3.0 Continue straight across a parking area and continue hiking on the signed Fall River Trail.

3.2 Arrive at a rock dam across the river and an end of trail sign. This is your turnaround point. Retrace the same route back to your starting point.

6.4 Arrive back at the trailhead.

10 Ray Atkeson Memorial Trail

This picturesque hike, named for the famed nature photographer, takes you along the shore of Sparks Lake and travels through a thick lodgepole pine forest and past interesting lava flows. Along the way, you'll have wonderful views of South Sister and Broken Top.

Distance: 2.3-mile loop.
Approximate hiking time: 1 hour.
Elevation gain: 60 feet.
Trail surface: Paved path, dirt path.
Best season: Late June through October.
Other trail users: None.
Canine compatibility: Leashed dogs permitted.

Fees and permits: A $5 Northwest Forest Pass is required. You can purchase a pass by calling (800) 270-7504 or online at www.naturenorthwest.org.
Schedule: Open all hours.
Maps: Maptech CD: Coos Bay/Eugene/Bend, OR.
USGS map: Broken Top, OR.

Finding the trailhead: From Bend travel 26 miles west on the Cascade Lakes Highway (Highway 46) to the turnoff for Forest Road 400 at the SPARKS LAKE RECREATION AREA sign. Turn left (south) on FR 400 and go 0.1 mile to a road junction. Bear left on Forest Road 100 toward the SPARKS LAKE BOAT RAMP AND TRAILHEADS sign. Go 1.7 miles and turn left into the Ray Atkeson Memorial Trailhead parking area. *DeLorme: Oregon Atlas & Gazetteer:* Page 50 D3.

The Hike

This short loop hike takes you through a scattered pine forest filled with interesting lava outcroppings. The trail begins by paralleling the shore of scenic Sparks Lake, which covers almost 400 acres and has an average depth of 10 feet. This

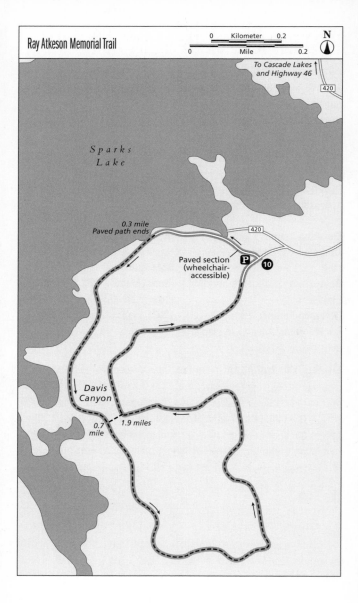

Ray Atkeson Memorial Trail

0   Kilometer   0.2

0   Mile   0.2

N

To Cascade Lakes
and Highway 46

420

*Sparks
Lake*

0.3 mile
Paved path ends

420

Paved section
(wheelchair-
accessible)

P   **10**

*Davis
Canyon*

0.7
mile

1.9 miles

lake was named for an early settler named Lige Sparks.

This high Cascade Lake is popular with canoeists and kayakers, who come here to paddle in its quiet waters and admire the stunning backdrop of the Three Sisters and Broken Top.

The route starts on a wheelchair-accessible path that follows the contours of the lava-strewn lakeshore. The paved path ends after 0.3 mile and becomes a dirt path. You'll follow this trail as it hugs the lakeshore and then weaves in and out of lava outcroppings and scattered pine trees for another 2.1 miles.

Miles and Directions

0.0   Start walking on the signed paved trail. Go 100 yards and turn right onto the signed barrier-free trail.

0.2   Enjoy a spectacular view of Sparks Lake and South Sister.

0.3   Pass a rest bench with a nice view of South Sister. About 100 yards past the bench, the paved path ends. Continue hiking on the signed hiking trail.

0.7   Continue straight on the signed hiking loop. (Note: The Davis Canyon Loop Trail goes left at this junction.)

1.4   Arrive at the top of a small knoll that provides a good viewpoint of Broken Top.

1.9   Continue straight (right) at the trail junction.

2.3   The trail turns from dirt to pavement. At a trail junction, continue to the right and arrive back at the trailhead in another 100 yards.

11 Green Lakes

This popular hike parallels enchanting Fall Creek and leads you to the Green Lakes Basin. You can admire this group of high Cascade lakes and also enjoy views of South Sister and Broken Top.

Distance: 9 miles out and back, with an 11-mile loop option.
Approximate hiking time: 4 to 5 hours.
Elevation gain: 1,100 feet.
Trail surface: Paved path, dirt path.
Best season: Late June through October.
Other trail users: None.
Canine compatibility: Leashed dogs permitted.

Fees and permits: A $5 Northwest Forest Pass is required. You can purchase a pass by calling (800) 270-7504 or online at www.naturenorthwest.org. A free wilderness permit is also required and is available at the trailhead.
Schedule: Open all hours.
Maps: Maptech CD: Coos Bay/Eugene/Bend, OR.
USGS map: Broken Top, OR.

Finding the trailhead: From the intersection of U.S. Highway 97 (Business) and Franklin Avenue in downtown Bend, turn west on Franklin Avenue. Proceed 1.2 miles (Franklin Avenue becomes Riverside Boulevard) to the intersection with Tumalo Avenue. Turn right onto Tumalo Avenue (which becomes Galveston Avenue). Go 0.5 mile and turn left onto Fourteenth Street. This street soon becomes Century Drive, also known as the Cascade Lakes Highway (Highway 46). Continue about 27 miles on the highway to the Green Lakes trailhead parking area on the right side of the road. *DeLorme: Oregon Atlas and Gazetteer:* Page 50 D3.

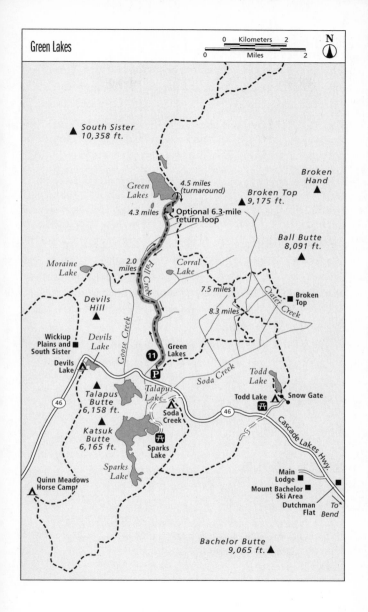

Green Lakes

0   Kilometers   2

0   Miles   2

N

▲ South Sister
10,358 ft.

Broken
Hand ▲

Green
Lakes

4.5 miles
(turnaround)

Broken Top
▲ 9,175 ft.

4.3 miles

Optional 6.3-mile
return loop

Ball Butte
8,091 ft.
▲

Moraine
Lake

2.0
miles

Fall Creek

Corral
Lake

7.5 miles

Outlet Creek

Broken
Top ■

Devils
Hill ▲

8.3 miles

Goose Creek

Wickiup
Plains and
South Sister ■

Devils
Lake

Green
Lakes

11 P

Todd
Lake

Devils
Lake ▲

Talapus
Lake

Soda Creek

Todd Lake ▲

Snow Gate ●

46

Talapus
Butte
6,158 ft. ▲

Soda
Creek

46

Cascade Lakes Hwy.

Katsuk
Butte
6,165 ft. ▲

Sparks
Lake

Sparks
Lake

Main
Lodge ■

Mount Bachelor
Ski Area ■

Quinn Meadows
Horse Camp ▲

Dutchman
Flat ■

To
Bend

Bachelor Butte
9,065 ft. ▲

The Hike

This popular route takes you on a tour of the Three Sisters Wilderness along the banks of charming Fall Creek. This boulder-strewn creek is filled with beautiful waterfalls around almost every bend. You'll follow the wide, dirt path along the banks of the creek through fragrant forest. The trail also affords views of the Newberry Lava Flow, which erupted from the southeast side of South Sister—youngest of the Three Sisters volcanoes. Shiny, black obsidian is present in this amazing lava flow. Because of how obsidian is formed (through rapid cooling of lava), it is very hard and extremely sharp. These properties were highly valued by Native Americans, who called the rock Isukws (pronounced "eshookwsh") and used it to make arrowheads, knives, jewelry, ornaments, sculptures, ceremonial objects, and tools.

After 4.3 miles you'll enter the magnificent Green Lakes Basin. Three greenish-colored lakes fill the basin. Enjoy views of the lakes, South Sister, and Broken Top, and return on the same route. If you are feeling ambitious and want to return on the trail via a loop route, follow the Soda Creek Trail 6.3 miles back to the trailhead. See the "Miles and Directions" section for details. Be sure to arm yourself with mosquito repellent on this hike.

Miles and Directions

0.0   Start hiking on smooth wide Trail #17, which parallels Fall Creek. A sign at the start of the trail indicates MORAINE LAKE 2 MILES/GREEN LAKES 4.5 MILES/PARK MEADOW 9 MILES/SCOTT PASS 21 MILES. The route parallels Fall Creek, which has beautiful waterfalls around almost every bend.

2.0   Arrive at a trail junction. Continue straight (right) on the smooth track as it parallels Fall Creek. (The trail that goes left at this junction heads toward Moraine Lake.)

4.3   You'll arrive at the Park Meadow/Soda Creek Trail junction. Continue straight to enter the Green Lakes Basin.

4.5   Enjoy views of the lakes and then turn around and return on the same route.

9.0   Arrive back at the trailhead.

Loop Option: To complete a loop back to the trailhead, you can return on a 6.3-mile route via the Soda Creek Trail. Turn right at the junction at Mile 4.3 toward Park Meadow/Soda Creek. Walk 10 yards and then take another quick right turn toward Soda Creek/Broken Top. Continue climbing up the trail and enjoy awesome views of the Green Lakes to the north. The route skirts the south edge of the 9,175-foot Broken Top peak.

7.5   Turn right toward Soda Creek/Todd Lake. (The Broken Top Trail continues left at this junction.)

8.3   Turn right where a sign indicates SODA CREEK. (The trail that goes left heads toward Todd Lake.) From here you'll continue downhill—be ready to negotiate water crossings at Crater and Soda Creeks.

11.0   Arrive back at the Green Lakes trailhead.

12 Osprey Point

This route takes you to a spectacular viewpoint of Crane Prairie Reservoir, where you may see ospreys fishing in the productive waters of the reservoir. You also have the option to take a side trip to view the historic Billy Quinn gravesite.

Distance: 0.7-mile loop.
Approximate hiking time: 30 minutes.
Elevation gain: None.
Trail surface: Paved path, dirt path.
Best season: Late June through October.
Other trail users: None.
Canine compatibility: Leashed dogs permitted.

Fees and permits: A $5 Northwest Forest Pass is required. You can purchase a pass by calling (800) 270-7504 or online at www.naturenorthwest.org. A free wilderness permit is also required and is available at the trailhead.
Schedule: Open all hours.
Maps: Maptech CD: Coos Bay/ Eugene/Bend, OR.
USGS map: Crane Prairie Reservoir, OR.

Finding the trailhead: From Bend, travel west and then south for 50.1 miles on the Cascade Lakes Highway (Highway 46) to a turnoff on the left side for the Osprey Point Interpretive Trail. Turn left and continue a short distance to a road fork. Turn left and continue 0.1 mile to a gravel parking area and the trailhead. *DeLorme: Oregon Atlas & Gazetteer:* Page 44 B2.

The Hike

This short loop hike gives you the opportunity to look for ospreys hunting and feeding in Crane Prairie Reservoir. The

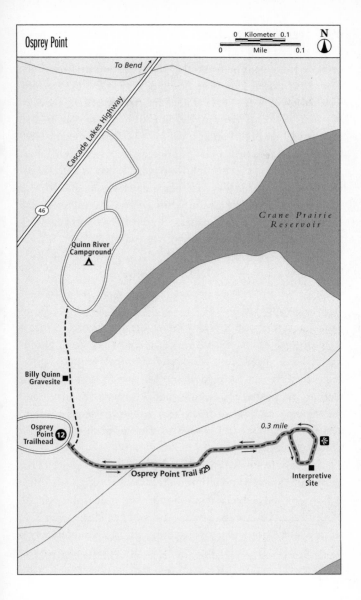

Osprey Point

To Bend

Cascade Lakes Highway

46

Crane Prairie
Reservoir

Quinn River
Campground

Billy Quinn
Gravesite

Osprey Point
Trailhead 12

0.3 mile

Interpretive
Site

Osprey Point Trail #29

0   Kilometer   0.1

0   Mile   0.1

N

reservoir was originally built in 1920 with private funds. In 1940 the Bureau of Reclamation rebuilt the reservoir to provide irrigation for Central Oregon farmers and ranchers. The dam caused extensive flooding and killed many trees. The dead tree snags provide ideal habitat for nesting ospreys. Related to both hawks and eagles, ospreys are classified in their own family, Pandionidae. These magnificent birds weigh up to four and a half pounds and have a 6-foot wingspan. They have striking yellow-orange eyes and a predominantly white underside with black markings on the top of their wings. Their heads are white, with a distinctive black band across the eyes and cheeks. So distinctive and beautiful, their plumage was once used to trim women's hats.

Also known as the fish hawk, the osprey's diet is made up almost entirely of fish. The osprey has the ability to reverse its outer claw, having talons facing both forward and backward so that it can more easily hold on to its catch. It can also spot fish from as high as 90 feet. Once it spots a good catch, it'll make a fast, arrowlike dive, plunging as far as 4 feet into the water. Ospreys migrate to the high lakes area in early April and lay two to four eggs. The eggs are incubated for twenty-eight to thirty-five days, and the osprey chicks stay in the nest for up to ten weeks. In October the adults and young migrate south to Central and South America.

The trail weaves through a thick lodgepole pine forest. Listen for squirrels and chipmunks as well as songbirds. After 0.3 mile you'll arrive at a junction to begin the loop portion of the hike. Interpretive signs and rest benches invite you to stop and enjoy your surroundings. In late summer, when the water levels are lower, you have the option to hike out into a lush meadow on a primitive trail to the water's edge, where you'll have nice views of Mount Bachelor, Broken Top, and the Three Sisters to the north. After enjoying the views, head back to the main loop trail. Finish the loop and retrace the same route back to the trailhead.

Miles and Directions

0.0 Start walking on the Osprey Point Trail #29. (**Option:** Turn left and walk 0.1 mile to the Billy Quinn gravesite.)

0.3 Arrive at a T junction. Turn right to begin a short loop. From a viewpoint on the loop trail, look for ospreys fishing in the reservoir. (**Option:** If the water level is low, hike out through a lush meadow to the water's edge.)

0.4 The loop portion of the trail ends. Follow the main trail back to the trailhead.

0.7 Arrive back at the trailhead.

Sisters

13 **Park Meadow**

This hike takes you into a high alpine meadow in the Three Sisters Wilderness with gorgeous views of Broken Top and South Sister.

Distance: 7.2 miles out and back.

Approximate hiking time: 2½ to 3½ hours.

Elevation gain: 700 feet.

Trail surface: Dirt path.

Best season: Late June through October.

Other trail users: Equestrians.

Canine compatibility: Leashed dogs permitted.

Fees and permits: A $5 Northwest Forest Pass is required. You can purchase a pass by calling (800) 270-7504 or online at www.naturenorthwest.org. A free wilderness permit is also required. The self-issue permit can be obtained at the permit station, located on the trail 0.8 mile from the trailhead.

Schedule: Open all hours.

Maps: Maptech CD: Coos Bay/ Eugene/Bend, OR.

USGS map: Broken, OR.

Finding the trailhead: From U.S. Highway 20 in Sisters, turn south onto Elm Street (this street becomes Forest Road 16) and travel 14 miles to the Park Meadow trailhead on the right side of the road. Turn right at the trailhead sign onto a rough gravel road. (If you are driving a passenger car, you'll need to be careful when driving on this rocky, rutted road.) If you are in a passenger car, you can travel for 1 mile on this dirt road and park beside the road. You can then walk the remaining 0.1 mile to the trailhead. If you have a high-clearance vehicle, you can drive the 1.1 miles to the trailhead. *DeLorme: Oregon Atlas & Gazetteer:* Page 50 C3.

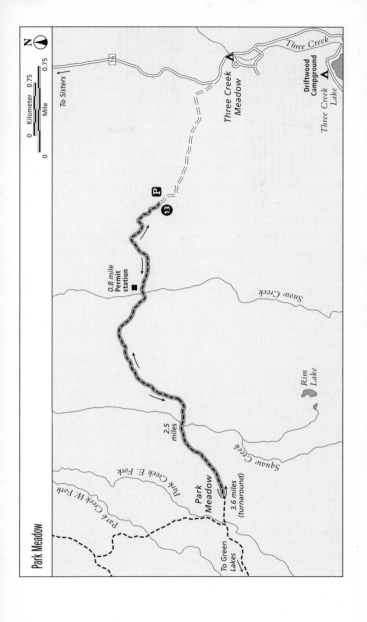

Park Meadow

N

0   Kilometer   0.75
0   Mile   0.75

To Sisters

16

Three Creek

Three Creek Meadow

Driftwood Campground

Three Creek Lake

P

13

0.8 mile Permit station

Snow Creek

Rim Lake

Squaw Creek

2.5 miles

Park Creek E. Fork

Park Creek W. Fork

Park Meadow

3.6 miles (turnaround)

To Green Lakes

The Hike

This route begins by winding through a thick forest of mountain hemlock, cedar, and blue spruce. Mountain hemlock can be found growing at elevations of 3,500 to 6,000 feet and is often confused with western hemlock. This hardy tree differs from the western hemlock by having thick needles that fan out in bushy clusters. It also has 2-inch-long cones and blue-green foliage. In contrast, the western hemlock has flat needles that are shaped in an open spray, cones that are an inch or less in length, and yellow-green foliage. Mountain hemlocks are also characterized by their deep, furrowed bark and are usually the first trees to grow at timberline. It's not uncommon for a mature branch to touch the ground and take root as a new tree. The parent tree then shelters the new tree from the harsh high-altitude environment.

Be sure to obtain a wilderness permit at the self-issue station at 0.8 mile. After walking for about 2 miles, you'll get sneak peeks of Broken Top and South Sister above the tree line. At 2.5 miles, cross a log bridge over bubbling Squaw Creek—a major source of irrigation for Central Oregon farmers and ranchers. After 3.4 miles arrive at Park Meadow, where you'll have unsurpassed views of Broken Top and South Sister from the gorgeous wildflower-filled meadow. Continue walking through the meadow to your turnaround point at 3.6 miles. (Note: Be sure to arm yourself with mosquito repellent on this hike.)

Miles and Directions

0.0   Start hiking at the trailhead sign that indicates PARK MEADOW 3.75/GREEN LAKES TRAIL 6.75.

0.8	Cross a shallow stream and then arrive at a four-way junction. Continue straight toward Park Meadow. Be sure to pick up a free self-issue wilderness permit at the permit station at this junction.
1.2	Cross a log bridge over a bubbling creek. Continue hiking on the forested trail, which has periodic rocky sections.
2.5	Cross a log bridge over Squaw Creek.
3.4	Arrive at Park Meadow. To continue across the meadow, cross a log bridge over a fast-flowing creek and continue on the trail across the meadow for about another 0.2 mile.
3.6	Arrive at the route's turnaround point. Be sure to bask in the sun and enjoy the spectacular mountain views before retracing your route to your starting point.
7.2	Arrive back at the trailhead.

14 Squaw Creek Falls

This hike takes you to a viewpoint of the swirling cascade of Squaw Creek Falls in Deschutes National Forest.

Distance: 1.8 miles out and back.
Approximate hiking time: 1 hour.
Elevation gain: 200 feet.
Trail surface: Dirt path.
Best season: June through October.
Other trail users: None.
Canine compatibility: Dogs permitted.
Fees and permits: A $5 North-

west Forest Pass is required. You can purchase a pass by calling (800) 270-7504 or online at www.naturenorthwest.org. A free wilderness permit is also required and can be obtained at the trailhead.
Schedule: Open all hours.
Maps: Maptech CD: Coos Bay/Eugene/Bend, OR.
USGS map: Trout Creek Butte, OR.

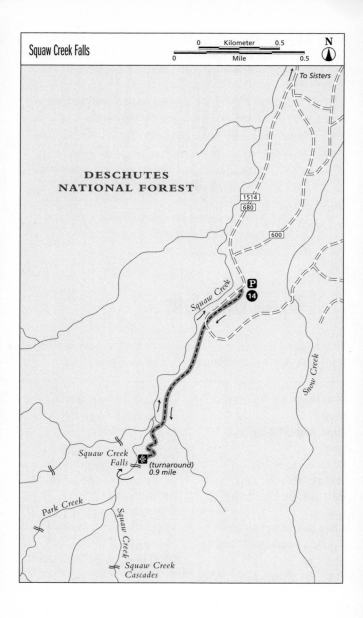

0   Kilometer   0.5

0   Mile   0.5

N

**DESCHUTES
NATIONAL FOREST**

To Sisters

1514
680

600

Squaw Creek

P
14

Snow Creek

Squaw Creek
Falls

(turnaround)
0.9 mile

Park Creek

Squaw Creek

Squaw Creek
Cascades

Finding the trailhead: From U.S. Highway 20 in Sisters, turn south onto Elm Street (Forest Road 16) and travel 7.5 miles south. Turn right onto Forest Road 1514 (a gravel, washboard road), where a sign indicates SQUAW CREEK 5 MILES. Continue 5.1 miles to the junction with Forest Road 1514-600 and turn left. Use caution, as this road is very rough. Continue 2.3 miles to the junction with Forest Road 1514-680 and turn left (south). Travel 0.4 mile on this rough road to the trailhead. *DeLorme: Oregon Atlas & Gazetteer:* Page 50 C3.

The Hike

Start hiking on this dirt path as it travels through a thick lodgepole pine forest. Straight and slender, lodgepole pines grow in thick stands and are distinguished by their prickly cones and pairs of 2-inch-long needles.

After 0.5 mile you'll cross a small stream. If you have your dog with you, this is a good place to let him cool off. After a short 0.9 mile, you'll arrive at a nice viewpoint of Squaw Creek Falls. The fanlike cascade tumbles about 30 feet over large boulders before continuing its journey down the canyon. You can descend on a short, rough trail to the water's edge if you want a closer look at this impressive cascade. Return on the same route.

Miles and Directions

0.0   Start hiking on the dirt path.
0.5   Cross a small stream.
0.9   Arrive at a viewpoint of Squaw Creek Falls. Retrace the same route back to the trailhead.
1.8   Arrive back at the trailhead.

15 Head of the Metolius River

This popular route takes you to a spectacular viewpoint of the natural spring that is the source for the Metolius River.

Distance: 0.5 mile out and back.
Approximate hiking time: 30 minutes.
Elevation gain: None.
Trail surface: Paved path.
Best season: Open year round. Snow may be present during the winter months.
Other trail users: None.

Canine compatibility: Leashed dogs permitted.
Fees and permits: No fees or permits required.
Schedule: Open all hours.
Maps: Maptech CD: Coos Bay/Eugene/Bend, OR.
USGS map: Black Butte, OR.

Finding the trailhead: From Sisters travel 10 miles west on U.S. Highway 20 to the junction with Forest Road 14. Turn right onto FR 14 toward Camp Sherman. Continue 2.8 miles to a Y junction. Turn right toward the signed campgrounds. Continue 1.6 miles and turn left onto Forest Road 1400–140. Continue 0.1 mile to a paved parking area and the trailhead. *DeLorme: Oregon Atlas & Gazetteer:* Page 50 A3.

The Hike

This short hike follows a wide paved path to a bubbling spring that is the source of the Metolius River. Picnic tables and restrooms are located at the trailhead. Many visitors hike this short route and then eat lunch underneath the shady canopy of the towering ponderosa pines.

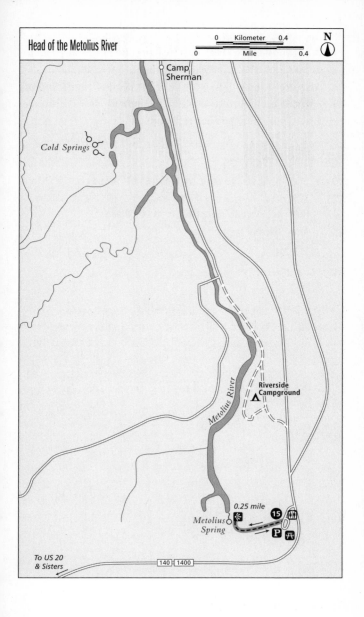

Head of the Metolius River

N

0   Kilometer   0.4
0   Mile   0.4

Camp Sherman

Cold Springs

Metolius River

Riverside Campground

0.25 mile

Metolius Spring

15

P

140 1400

To US 20 & Sisters

The path is framed with a decorative split-rail fence and travels through a parklike stand of ponderosa pine trees to a viewpoint of the Metolius Spring. From the viewpoint you'll have a stunning view of a grassy meadow, with snow-capped Mount Jefferson in the background. You'll retrace the same route back to the trailhead.

Miles and Directions

0.0   Start hiking on the wheelchair-accessible paved path.

0.25   Arrive at a viewpoint of the headwaters of the Metolius River. Retrace the same route back to the trailhead.

0.5   Arrive back at the trailhead.

16 West Metolius River

This unique trail traces the banks of the clear, fast-moving Metolius River and meanders through a lush riparian eco-system of bright wildflowers and riverside vegetation. The spring-fed river rushes over lava to create swirling rapids and big eddies that are home to various species of trout. At the turnaround point is Wizard Falls Fish Hatchery, home to millions of eastern brook trout, German brown trout, and rainbow trout.

Distance: 5.0 miles out and back (with longer options).

Approximate hiking time: 2 to 3 hours.

Elevation gain: 200 feet.

Trail surface: Dirt path.

Best season: Open year round. The driest months are June through October.

Other trail users: None.

Canine compatibility: Leashed dogs permitted.

Fees and permits: No fees or permits required.

Schedule: Open all hours.

Maps: Maptech CD: Coos Bay/ Eugene/Bend, OR.

USGS maps: Black Butte, OR; Candle Creek, OR; Prairie Farm Spring, OR.

Finding the trailhead: From Sisters head 10 miles west on U.S. Highway 20 to Camp Sherman Road (Forest Road 14). Turn right (north) and travel 2.7 miles to the junction with Forest Road 1419. Turn left and go 2.3 miles to another road junction and stop sign. Continue straight (you're now on Forest Road 1420) for another 3.4 miles to the junction with Forest Road 400. Turn right onto FR 400 toward Lower Canyon Creek Campground; go 0.9 mile through the campground to the road's end and trailhead. *DeLorme: Oregon Atlas & Gazetteer:* Page 50 A3.

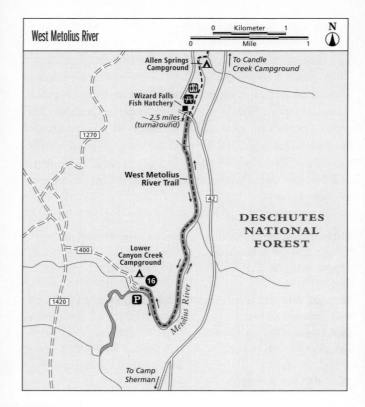

0   Kilometer   1

0   Mile   1

West Metolius River

Allen Springs
Campground

*To Candle
Creek Campground*

Wizard Falls
Fish Hatchery

*~2.5 miles
(turnaround)*

West Metolius
River Trail

42

DESCHUTES
NATIONAL
FOREST

1270

400

Lower
Canyon Creek
Campground

16

1420

P

Metolius River

*To Camp
Sherman*

N

The Hike

The Metolius River, known for its world-class fly-fishing, originates as a natural spring at the base of Black Butte before winding its way north through the Metolius Basin and into Lake Billy Chinook. Numerous springs, fed via porous volcanic rock high in the Central Cascade Mountains, continue to feed the river along its length, keeping the flow rate fairly steady at 1,200 to 1,800 cubic feet per second.

Homesteading in the Metolius Valley didn't occur until 1881. Settlers were attracted to the area by the thick timber and abundant grass that provided good grazing for livestock. The numerous springs and creeks in the valley also provided a plentiful supply of water. In 1893, with the passage of the Forest Reserve Act by President Grover Cleveland, the Metolius Valley became part of the Cascade Range Forest Reserve. In 1908 the area was incorporated into Deschutes National Forest.

If you want to explore this beautiful river, the West Metolius River Trail is the easiest way to do it. The trail starts at Lower Canyon Creek Campground, located approximately 20 miles northwest of Sisters, and continues on a scenic journey to Wizard Falls Fish Hatchery. Along the way there is lush streamside greenery (including pinkish-lavender streambank globemallow and bright orange fragrant honeysuckle) as well as open forest dotted with purple lupine, crimson columbine, lavender-tufted thistle, and white-headed yarrow. Large ponderosa pines shade the path, and the river's deep rock pools and logs provide a haven for trout. After 2.5 miles the trail arrives at Wizard Falls Fish Hatchery, which has water and restrooms. This is a great place to rest before the return trip to the trailhead.

Miles and Directions

0.0 Start this river hike at the WOOD WEST METOLIUS RIVER TRAIL sign located in the Lower Canyon Creek Campground. A sign indicates that you'll reach Wizard Falls in 2.5 miles.

0.3 Look off to the right to view an amazing natural spring that splashes into the river from underground.

2.5 Arrive at Wizard Falls Fish Hatchery. If you are feeling curious, take the time to explore the fish hatchery before you head back to the trailhead. Water and restrooms are available here. (**Option:** If you want to enjoy a longer river route, you can continue on the trail on the west or east side of the river for about 5 more miles.)

5.0 Arrive back at the trailhead.

17 Little Belknap Crater

This stretch of the Pacific Crest Trail traverses rock-strewn, moonlike terrain on its way to the summit of Little Belknap Crater. Along the way you'll pass lava rock, lava tubes, and fascinating caves. And from the summit you can enjoy views of the Three Sisters, Mount Washington, Black Crater, and many other Cascade peaks.

Distance: 7.2 miles out and back (with longer options).

Approximate hiking time: 3 to 4 hours.

Elevation gain: 975 feet.

Trail surface: Dirt path and lava scree.

Best season: July through October.

Other trail users: None.

Canine compatibility: Dogs permitted. However, this hike is not recommended for dogs due to the sharp lava scree, which can cut your dog's feet, and no access to shade or water.

Fees and permits: A free self-issue wilderness permit is required and is available at the trailhead.

Schedule: Open all hours.

Maps: Maptech CD: Coos Bay/Eugene/Bend, OR.

USGS map: Mount Washington, OR.

Finding the trailhead: From Sisters travel 14.9 miles west on the McKenzie Highway (Highway 242) to the Pacific Crest Trail #2000 trailhead, located on the right (north) side of the road. (A very small hiker sign marks the trailhead.) Note: Depending on the winter snow conditions, the McKenzie Highway may not open until mid-July. *DeLorme: Oregon Atlas & Gazetteer:* Page 50 B2.

The Hike

The rugged character of Central Oregon's lava country is nowhere better represented than on this hike to the summit

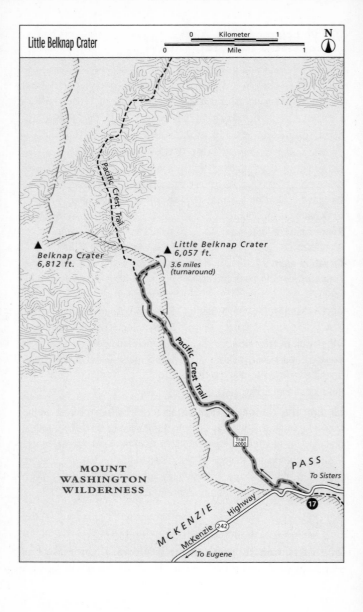

Little Belknap Crater

0 — Kilometer — 1
0 — Mile — 1

N

Pacific Crest Trail

Belknap Crater
6,812 ft.

Little Belknap Crater
6,057 ft.
3.6 miles
(turnaround)

Pacific Crest Trail

Trail
2000

MOUNT
WASHINGTON
WILDERNESS

PASS
To Sisters

17

McKenzie Highway

MCKENZIE
McKenzie Highway 242
To Eugene

of Little Belknap Crater. The rich history of the area begins with the highway to the trailhead. The McKenzie Highway (Highway 242) is a gorgeous scenic byway with spectacular views of mountains, lava fields, and endless blue sky—a great introduction to the hike you're about to take. When gold was discovered in eastern Oregon and Idaho in the 1860s, settlers made a push to find a route that connected the Willamette Valley on the west side of the Cascades to the land on the east. In 1862 Felix Scott and his brother Marion led a party of forty men, sixty oxen, and 900 head of cattle and horses across McKenzie Pass, blazing what would later become the Scott Trail.

An extremely rough trail, the Scott Trail required almost five days to travel from Eugene in the Willamette Valley to the small town of Sisters in Central Oregon. For future travelers a toll road was built in 1872 that traveled up Lost Creek Canyon, traversed over the rough lava beds, and ended at the Deschutes River.

The trail (95 percent of which follows the Pacific Crest Trail) leads through the heart of the Mount Washington Wilderness and its rugged lava formations, craters, and extinct volcanoes. The route begins rather innocently as it winds through an open forest. But within a mile, things change drastically. Soon the forest is replaced by a grayish-black lava flow practically devoid of life, except for the rare hardy tree that has managed to sink its roots through the jumbled basalt rocks.

The flow was created more than 2,900 years ago when hot liquid basalt poured from Belknap Crater, the large cinder cone to the west. Approximately twenty years later a second eruption sprung from out of Little Belknap Crater, located directly north of the trailhead. A third phase of eruptions occurred a little more than a thousand years later from the northeast base of Belknap Crater, releasing lava 9 miles west into the McKenzie River Valley.

After 3 miles of hiking through this mysterious maze of rock, you'll come to a trail junction and go right. In 0.3 mile you'll pass a deep lava tube on your left. If you approach the edge of the tube and look in (be careful—it's quite a drop-off), you can feel the cool air escaping from deep within the earth.

From the lava tube, hike a steep and dramatic 0.1 mile to the top of Little Belknap Crater. The trail surface is loose and crumbly, and piles of gray rock mingle with the bright red cinders that form much of the crater. When you reach the top you can enjoy magnificent views of Belknap Crater, Mount Washington, Black Crater, and the Three Sisters Mountains. The summit of Little Belknap Crater is your turnaround point.

Miles and Directions

0.0 Start hiking on the signed Pacific Crest Trail #2000. (Note: Be sure to fill out the free self-issue wilderness permit at the trailhead.)

1.0 Begin walking on the lava flow.

3.2 Come to a trail junction and turn right to hike to the summit of Little Belknap Crater.

3.5 Pass a lava tube on your left.

3.6 Reach the summit and enjoy sweeping views of Belknap Crater, Mount Washington, Black Crater, and the Three Sisters. Turn around here and retrace your route back to the trailhead. (**Option:** You can continue north on the Pacific Crest Trail and explore more of the Mount Washington Wilderness.)

7.2 Arrive back at the trailhead.

18 Hand Lake

This short, scenic route takes you to a small alpine lake, with gorgeous views of snowcapped Mount Washington.

Distance: 1.0 mile out and back.

Approximate hiking time: 30 minutes to 1 hour.

Elevation gain: 100 feet.

Trail surface: Dirt path.

Best season: July through October.

Other trail users: None.

Canine compatibility: Dogs permitted.

Fees and permits: A free self-issue wilderness permit is required and is available at the trailhead.

Schedule: Open all hours.

Maps: Maptech CD: Coos Bay/Eugene/Bend, OR.

USGS map: North Sister, OR.

Finding the trailhead: From Sisters, turn west onto the McKenzie Highway (Highway 242) and travel 19.3 miles to a gravel pullout on the left side of the road, marked by a brown hiker symbol. *DeLorme: Oregon Atlas & Gazetteer:* Page 50 B2.

The Hike

Begin this hike by crossing the highway (use caution) to the signed trailhead. Start hiking on the dirt path as it descends through a thick stand of lodgepole pine dotted with purple lupine. After 0.5 mile you'll emerge from the woods into a scenic high alpine meadow.

Take time to explore the rustic three-sided wood shelter and to walk on a side trail down to the lake's edge. From here you'll have outstanding views of the pointy summit of Mount Washington. Retrace the same route back to the trailhead. Be armed with mosquito repellent on this hike.

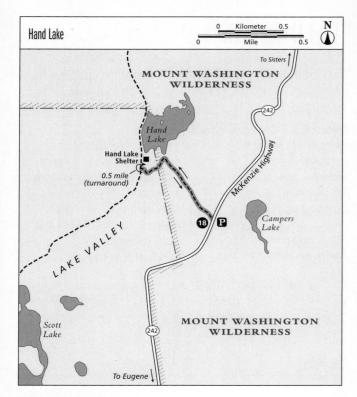

Miles and Directions

0.0   Cross Highway 242 and fill out a free wilderness permit at the signed trailhead. Start walking on the dirt path.

0.5   Arrive at a three-sided wood shelter. Follow a side trail down to the lake's edge. Retrace the same route back to the trailhead.

1.0   Arrive back at the trailhead.

19 Canyon Creek Meadows Loop

This very popular loop route takes you on a tour of a high alpine meadow, with bubbling Canyon Creek flowing through it. In addition, you'll enjoy spectacular views of the jagged spires of Three Fingered Jack.

Distance: 5.5-mile loop.
Approximate hiking time: 2½ to 3½ hours.
Elevation gain: 675 feet.
Trail surface: Dirt path.
Best season: Late June through October.
Other trail users: None.
Canine compatibility: Leashed dogs permitted.
Fees and permits: A $5 Northwest Forest Pass is required.

You can purchase a pass at the entrance booth to the monument, online at www.naturenorthwest.org, or by calling (800) 270-7504. A free self-issue wilderness permit is also required and is available at the trailhead.
Schedule: Open all hours.
Maps: Maptech CD: Coos Bay/Eugene/Bend, OR.
USGS maps: Three Fingered Jack, OR; Marion Lake, OR.

Finding the trailhead: From Sisters head west on U.S. Highway 20 for 12 miles to Jack Lake Road (Forest Road 12). Turn right and travel 4.3 miles on Jack Lake Road to the junction with Forest Road 1230. Turn left onto FR 1230 and go 1.7 miles. Turn left onto Forest Road 1234 (the road becomes gravel here) and travel about 6.2 more miles to Jack Lake and the trailhead. DeLorme: *Oregon Atlas & Gazetteer:* Page 50 A2.

The Hike

High mountain scenery is the highlight of this popular trail. The route takes you past Jack Lake and then enters spectacular Canyon Creek Meadows. This small lake covers about seven acres and hosts a nice campground.

After 0.2 mile you'll arrive in a high alpine meadow that has a profusion of bright purple lupine and brilliant red Indian paintbrush blooms in summer. After 2 miles you'll enjoy a stunning view of the craggy spires of 7,841-foot Three Fingered Jack—named in honor of Joaquin Murietta, an aspiring gold rusher with a mutilated, three-fingered hand. The spires rise abruptly out of Central Oregon's Mount Jefferson Wilderness to form a geologic slice of time. Hundreds of thousands of years ago, the mountain—formed by hot basaltic lava flows—resembled a broad, dome-shaped cone. Since that time, volcanic activity and glaciation have left the southern side of the peak a skeleton of its previous majesty. Today the formation is what geologists call a shield volcano. After enjoying views of Three Fingered Jack, you'll continue on the loop route for another 2.3 miles until you end the loop at 5.3 miles. At the end of the loop, you'll return 0.2 mile to the trailhead.

Bring plenty of mosquito repellent with you on this hike. Also, try to hike this trail during the week to avoid the weekend crowds.

Canyon Creek Meadows Loop

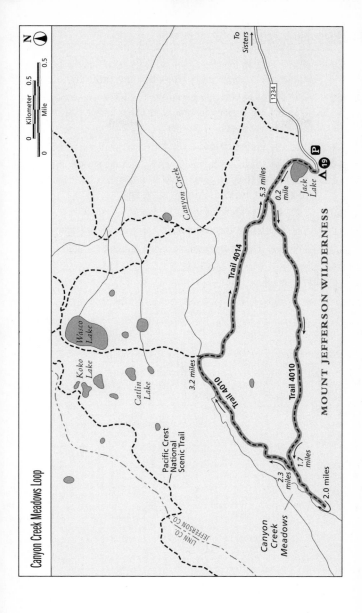

Miles and Directions

0.0   Start hiking on the singletrack trail signed for Canyon Creek Meadows. This trail travels past quiet Jack Lake.

0.2   Turn left toward Canyon Creek. The trail leads you into an amazing high alpine meadow filled with bubbling creeks and colorful wildflowers.

1.7   Turn left at the trail fork.

2.0   Arrive at a high alpine meadow with a stunning view of 7,841-foot Three Fingered Jack. After admiring the view, turn around and head back on the same trail.

2.3   Turn left at the trail junction.

3.2   Turn right at the trail junction.

5.3   Continue straight (left) toward Jack Lake and the trailhead.

5.5   Arrive back at the trailhead.

20 Lava River Trail–Dee Wright Observatory

This route explores the moonlike landscape of the Yapoah Crater Lava Flow in the Mount Washington Wilderness. As an added bonus, you can explore the unique Dee Wright Observatory.

Distance: 0.5-mile loop.
Approximate hiking time: 30 minutes to 1 hour.
Elevation gain: 200 feet.
Trail surface: Paved path.
Best season: July through October.
Other trail users: None.

Canine compatibility: Leashed dogs permitted.
Fees and permits: No fees or permits required.
Schedule: Open all hours.
Maps: Maptech CD: Coos Bay/Eugene/Bend, OR.
USGS map: Mount Washington, OR.

Finding the trailhead: From Sisters travel west on Highway 242 (the McKenzie Highway) for 14.4 miles to a paved parking area on the left side of the road. *DeLorme: Oregon Atlas & Gazetteer:* Page 50 B2.

The Hike

This hike explores the western edge of the Yapoah Crater Lava Flow. This incredible lava flow, 8 miles long and a mile wide, is thought to have erupted from Yapoah Crater as recently as 2,700 years ago. The lava that makes up this flow is called AA lava (pronounced *Ah-Ah*) or black lava. This type of lava is made up of basalt and has a rough, jagged surface. This rough surface is caused when the upper layers of lava cool quickly, while the lower layers are still flowing.

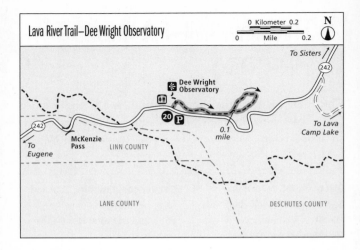

Lava River Trail–Dee Wright Observatory

You'll follow the paved path through the lava flow on a short 0.5-mile loop. When you finish the loop you can explore the Dee Wright Observatory. The observatory was built by the Civilian Conservation Corps (CCC) and named for an early-1900s Forest Service packer and mountain guide. The observatory's arched windows frame eleven Cascade peaks.

Miles and Directions

0.0   Start the hike by crossing the highway and turning right on the paved Lava River Trail. (If you go left you can walk up a series of short switchbacks to view the Dee Wright Observatory.)

0.1   Turn left to begin the loop portion of the trail.

0.2   Pass a rest bench on the right.

0.3   Finish the loop. Go left to return to the trailhead.

0.5 Arrive back at your starting point. Continue straight and walk up the paved spiral path to view the Dee Wright Observatory. After enjoying the views, head back to the parking area.

21 Suttle Lake Loop

This hike parallels Suttle Lake in the Deschutes National Forest and offers sublime views of Mount Washington and Black Butte, plus many enticing swimming holes.

Distance: 3.6-mile loop.

Approximate hiking time: 1½ to 2 hours.

Elevation gain: 5 feet.

Trail surface: Dirt path, paved road.

Best season: May through November.

Other trail users: Mountain bikers.

Canine compatibility: Leashed dogs permitted.

Fees and permits: A $5 Northwest Forest Pass is required. You can purchase a pass online at www.naturenorthwest.org, or by calling (800) 270-7504.

Schedule: Open all hours.

Maps: Maptech CD: Coos Bay/ Eugene/Bend, OR.

USGS map: Black Butte, OR.

Finding the trailhead: From Sisters, travel 12.5 miles west on U.S. Highway 20. Turn left at the SUTTLE LAKE MARINA & RESORT sign onto the Suttle Lake entrance road. Take the first right turn, signed CINDER BEACH. Go 0.3 mile to a parking lot next to the lake and the trailhead. *DeLorme: Oregon Atlas & Gazetteer: Page 50 A3.*

The Hike

A glacier that extended to Mount Washington about 25,000 years ago formed Suttle Lake; you may notice its elongated shape and steep banks, typical of glacial lakes. Originally Suttle Lake was called Butte Lake by two early explorers named Andrew Wiley and John Gray, who sought a wagon route over the Cascades in 1859. This name didn't last long, however. In 1866 a pioneer named John Settle stumbled on the lake while on a hunting trip. Unaware of its existing name, he pridefully called it Settles. Suttle has since become the geographic name for the lake, most likely due to a spelling error.

This perfectly maintained trail around the lake is edged with such abundant vine maple that in autumn it displays an amazing show of oranges, reds, and bright yellows, contrasting sharply with the rest of the forest greenery. As you hike around the lake, it's easy to see why this lake has been a gathering place for people throughout history. The lake's gently sloping, sandy shores make great camping spots, and the lake's abundant fish make this a favorite hole for anglers. In 1925 Suttle Lake Lodge was built to accommodate the growing number of visitors frequenting the lake in the summer. The potential for winter recreation at Suttle Lake didn't go unnoticed either, and a ski hill was built southwest of the lake in the 1930s. In 1939 cross-country ski trails were cut in the Blue Lake/Suttle Lake area. Blue Lake, a close neighbor to Suttle Lake, is sometimes called the "Crater Lake of Central Oregon" due to its water's color. The striking blue color of the lake comes from its depth, more than 300 feet—a sharp contrast to Suttle Lake's paltry 75-foot depth. Unlike Suttle Lake's glacial history, Blue Lake was formed by a violent volcanic explosion about 1,500 years ago.

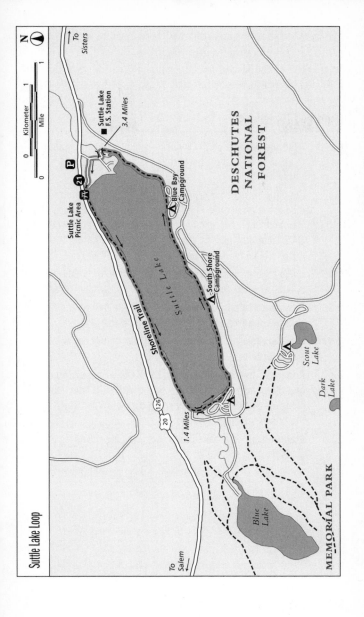

Suttle Lake Loop

In several places around the lake, you'll walk through camping, picnic, and swimming areas and will cross several boat ramps. Numerous access points along the shoreline are a sure sign of this lake's popularity during the summertime.

Miles and Directions

0.0 From the picnic area at Cinder Beach, start hiking around the lake in a counterclockwise direction on the signed Shoreline Trail.

1.4 Continue straight across a paved road at a boat ramp, and then cross an arched wood bridge over an outlet creek. After you cross the bridge, follow the trail as it hugs the shoreline. On a clear day, look for the pointy summit of Mount Washington above the tree line.

1.6 Cross a paved road and pick up the trail on the other side; continue on the smooth singletrack as it hugs the lakeshore.

2.5 Cross another paved road and pick up the trail on the other side, which takes you through a shady picnic area.

2.9 Cross another paved road and continue on the dirt path on the other side.

3.4 Arrive at a trail fork. Veer left at the SUTTLE TIE TRAILHEAD sign, and then cross a wood bridge over Link Creek. After you cross the bridge, take a very sharp right turn and watch for the brown trail signs.

3.5 Start walking on a paved road, following the brown trail signs marking the route.

3.6 Arrive back at the Cinder Beach parking area and your starting point.

22 Patjens Lakes Loop

This fun lake loop takes you on a tour of the Patjens Lakes and Big Lake in the Mount Washington Wilderness.

Distance: 6.2-mile loop.
Approximate hiking time: 3 to 4 hours.
Elevation gain: 400 feet.
Trail surface: Dirt path.
Best season: July through October.
Other trail users: None.
Canine compatibility: Dogs permitted.

Fees and permits: A free wilderness permit is required and is available at the trailhead.
Schedule: Open all hours.
Maps: Maptech CD: Coos Bay/Eugene/Bend, OR.
USGS maps: Clear Lake, OR; Mount Washington, OR.

Finding the trailhead: From Sisters, travel west on U.S. Highway 20 to the turnoff for Hoodoo Ski Bowl. Turn left (south) onto Big Lake Road and continue 4 miles to a dirt pullout and the trailhead on the right side of the road.

From Salem, follow Highway 22 east 82 miles to the junction with US 20. Stay left on US 20 toward Sisters and continue 6 miles to the turnoff for Hoodoo Ski Bowl. Turn right (south) onto Big Lake Road and continue 4 miles to a dirt pullout and the trailhead on the right side of the road. *DeLorme: Oregon Atlas & Gazetteer: Page 50 A1.*

The Hike

This hike offers nice views of the Three Sisters, Belknap Crater, and Mount Washington. At the trailhead, fill out a wilderness permit before you enter the Mount Washington Wilderness. Begin hiking on the Patjens Lake Trail 3395. The trail passes through a pine forest carpeted with clumps of bear grass and lupine. Early in the season, you'll pass small

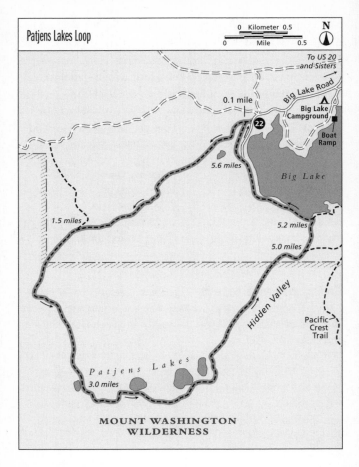

snowmelt ponds beginning at 0.8 mile. At 1.2 miles you'll ford a small creek. At 1.5 miles, stay left and continue on the main trail as it begins climbing over a low pass.

As you ascend, you'll have views over the trees of the Three Sisters and Belknap Crater. At 3.0 miles you'll arrive at a small lake on the right. A side trail leads to the lake's edge. As you continue you'll pass another lake on the left at 3.5 miles. A side trail heads down to the lake on the left. After 5.2 miles you'll arrive at scenic Big Lake. Big Lake covers approximately 225 acres and offers good fishing for kokanee, rainbow, and cutthroat trout. Enjoy the views of Hayrick Butte and the jagged summit of Mount Washington. At 6.1 miles you'll end the loop portion of the hike. Turn right and continue 0.1 mile back to the trailhead. If you want to explore this area more, you can set up camp at Big Lake Campground. Be armed with mosquito repellent on this hike.

Miles and Directions

0.0   Fill out a free wilderness permit at the trailhead and begin walking on the trail signed Patjens Lake Trail 3395.
0.1   Turn right at the trail fork to begin the loop.
1.2   Cross a small creek.
1.5   Turn left and ascend a small pass.
3.0   Pass a lake on the right. A side trail leads to the lake's edge.
3.5   Pass a lake on the left. A side trail leads to the lake's edge.
5.0   Turn left at the trail fork.
5.2   Arrive at Big Lake and stay to the left.
5.6   Turn left at the trail fork. The trail that heads right leads to Big Lake Campground.
6.1   End loop; turn right.
6.2   Arrive back at the trailhead.

Redmond

23 Smith Rock State Park

This route takes you on a scenic tour of the Crooked River Gorge in Smith Rock State Park. This gorge is surrounded by towering 400-foot cliffs and is filled with a variety of wildlife.

Distance: 3.2 miles out and back.

Approximate hiking time: 1½ to 2½ hours.

Elevation gain: 250 feet.

Trail surface: Dirt path.

Best season: April through October.

Other trail users: Mountain bikers and equestrians.

Canine compatibility: Leashed dogs permitted.

Fees and permits: A $3 day use permit is required and can be purchased at the self-pay station at the park. You can also purchase a day use permit or an annual Oregon State Parks permit for $25 by credit card by calling (800) 551-6949.

Schedule: Dawn to dusk.

Maps: Maptech CD: Coos Bay/ Eugene/Bend, OR.

USGS map: Redmond, OR.

Finding the trailhead: From Redmond drive approximately 4.5 miles north on U.S. Highway 97 to the small town of Terrebonne. At the flashing yellow light, turn right onto B Avenue (this becomes Smith Rock Way after the first stop sign). Drive 3.3 miles northeast, following the signs to Smith Rock State Park. *DeLorme: Oregon Atlas & Gazetteer:* Page 51 A7.

The Hike

Smith Rock is one of Central Oregon's most popular state parks. Before you even leave your car, you'll enjoy spectacular views of the park's colorful 400-foot-tall cliffs. These volcanic masterpieces started to take shape in the Miocene

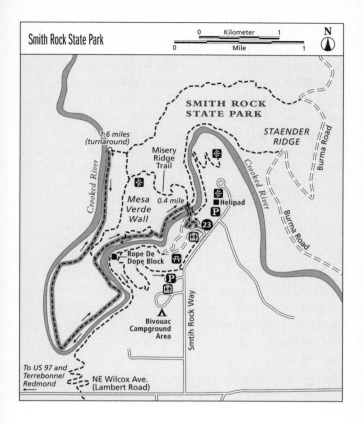

0   Kilometer   1

0   Mile   1

N

SMITH ROCK
STATE PARK

STAENDER
RIDGE

1.6 miles
(turnaround)

Misery
Ridge
Trail

Crooked River

Burma Road

Mesa
Verde
Wall

0.4 mile

Helipad

23

Rope De
Dope Block

Crooked River

Burma Road

P

Smtih Rock Way

Bivouac
Campground
Area

To US 97 and
Terrebonne/
Redmond

NE Wilcox Ave.
(Lambert Road)

period, nearly seventeen to nineteen million years ago, when hot steam and ash spewed from the ground. Traces of basalt can be found from the Newberry Volcano eruption 1.2 million years ago, which formed Paulina and East Lakes. Since this volcanic activity, the Crooked River has eroded the rock to form the columnar shapes that you see in the upper gorge today.

This 3.2-mile out-and-back hike begins with a steep descent to the canyon floor. A maintained viewpoint along the way is an excellent place to snap a photo and includes an interpretive sign describing the park's geologic history.

Upon reaching the canyon floor, the path crosses a bridge, turns left, and parallels the Crooked River. Along this stretch of the trail, watch for Canada geese, whose striking white throat patch and black head and neck make them easy to spot. The geese feed on the riverside vegetation and are apt to honk in alarm as you approach. Also keep an eye out for the river otters that are sometimes seen along this stretch of river. You'll also have plenty of opportunities to watch climbers clinging to the high cliff walls on the hundreds of climbing routes in the park.

After following the Crooked River for 1.6 miles on relatively flat terrain, you'll reach your turnaround point near the base of Monkey Face—a 350-foot-tall volcanic monolith with multiple climbing routes and an enormous cave. Look for climbers clinging to the wall's features as they attempt to reach the top of this amazing rock formation. Retrace the same route back to the trailhead.

This is just one of many hiking opportunities in this popular park.

Miles and Directions

0.0   From the parking area, head toward the canyon and take a right on an asphalt trail. Follow this to the canyon rim, where it begins its rough and raggedy spiral into Crooked River Canyon. After about 50 yards of careful descent, turn right onto a foot trail. Walk down this steep and rocky trail to the canyon floor.

0.4   Cross a footbridge over the Crooked River. After you cross the bridge, turn left where a sign notes that Morning Glory Wall is 0.25 mile and Monkey Face is 1.5 miles. Follow the trail as it follows the Crooked River. Enjoy the gorgeous canyon scenery and rock climbing action.

1.6   Arrive at a trail fork near the base of Monkey Face. Retrace the same route back to the trailhead.

3.2   Arrive back at the trailhead.

24 Gray Butte

This route travels through a fragrant sage-and-juniper landscape of the Crooked River National Grasslands. At the trail's turnaround point, you'll have grand views of the Central Cascade Mountains.

Distance: 3.8 miles out and back.

Approximate hiking time: 1½ to 2 hours.

Elevation gain: 200 feet.

Trail surface: Dirt path.

Best season: April through October.

Other trail users: Mountain bikers and equestrians.

Canine compatibility: Dogs permitted.

Fees and permits: No fees or permits required.

Schedule: Open all hours.

Maps: Maptech CD: Coos Bay/ Eugene/Bend, OR.

USGS map: Gray Butte, OR.

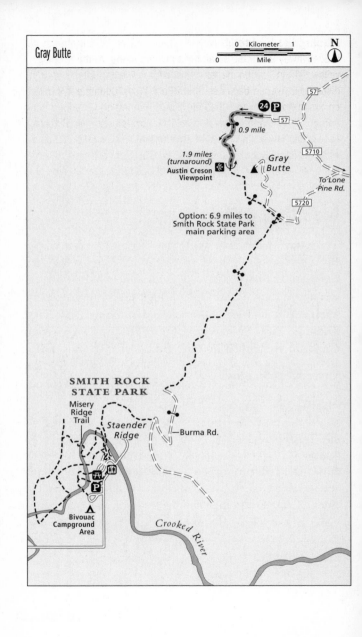

Finding the trailhead: From Redmond travel 4.5 miles north on U.S. Highway 97 to the small town of Terrebonne. At the flashing yellow light in Terrebonne, turn east onto B Avenue (after a short distance B Avenue becomes Smith Rock Way). Continue 4.9 miles on Smith Rock Way to Lone Pine Road. Turn left on Lone Pine Road and go 4.4 miles to Forest Road 5710. Turn left onto FR 5710 (you'll pass Skull Hollow Campground on your left). Follow FR 5710 as it winds up Skull Hollow Canyon for 2.6 miles. Turn left onto Forest Road 57. Continue 0.6 mile to a gravel pullout on the left side of the road. *DeLorme: Oregon Atlas & Gazetteer:* Page 51 B7.

The Hike

The Gray Butte Trail skirts the southwest edge of Gray Butte and travels through open grassland filled with fragrant sagebrush and juniper trees. This prominent butte rises 5,108 feet above the Central Oregon high desert and is part of a series of rounded buttes that provide a unique texture to the landscape. Gray Butte is part of the Crooked River National Grassland established in 1960. Although the grasslands are public property managed by the USDA Forest Service, large portions of the Crooked River National Grassland are open to range cattle from April through October.

After following the singletrack trail for 1.9 miles (and possibly dodging a few range cows), you'll arrive at a side trail on the right that leads to the Austin Creson Viewpoint. A memorial plaque for Austin Creson is located at this point and is dedicated to his hard work on planning the Gray Butte Trail. From the viewpoint you'll have spectacular views of the Three Sisters Mountains, Broken Top, Black Butte, and Mount Jefferson. After enjoying the views, retrace the same route back to the trailhead.

If you are feeling ambitious, you can continue 6.9 miles on the Gray Butte Trail to Smith Rock State Park.

Miles and Directions

0.0   The singletrack trail starts on the northeast edge of Gray Butte. The trail climbs slowly as it rounds the north edge of the butte.

0.9   Go through a green metal gate and continue your stroll through this magnificent high-desert landscape.

1.9   Turn right onto a side trail that leads to the Austin Creson Viewpoint. After enjoying the views, retrace the same route back to the trailhead. (**Option:** Continue 6.9 miles to the Smith Rock State Park main parking area. You can leave a car at Smith Rock and complete this as a shuttle hike.)

3.8   Arrive back at the trailhead.

25 Rimrock Springs Natural Area

This route takes you on a tour through the sagebrush-and-juniper landscape of the Rimrock Springs Natural Area, which contains a productive marsh where you can see geese, ducks, and other wildlife from a viewing platform.

Distance: 1.7-mile loop.
Approximate hiking time: 1 hour.
Elevation gain: 230 feet.
Trail surface: Paved path and dirt path.
Best season: Open year round.
Other trail users: None.

Canine compatibility: Dogs permitted.
Fees and permits: No fees or permits required.
Schedule: Open all hours.
Maps: Maptech CD: Coos Bay/Eugene/Bend, OR.
USGS map: Gray Butte, OR.

Rimrock Springs Natural Area

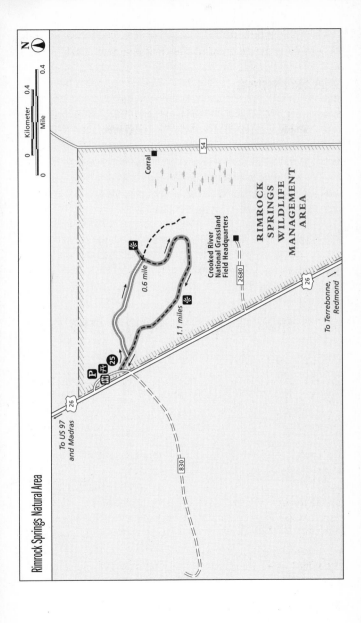

Finding the trailhead: From Redmond drive 5 miles north on U.S. Highway 97 to the small town of Terrebonne. At the flashing yellow light, turn right onto B Avenue (Smith Rock Way). Go 4.7 miles and turn left (north) onto Lone Pine Road. Continue 7.2 miles to the intersection with U.S. Highway 26. Turn left onto US 26 and go 4.4 miles to the parking area signed RIMROCK SPRINGS WILDLIFE MANAGEMENT AREA, located on the right side of the highway.

From Madras, drive south on US 97 for about 2 miles to a sign that indicates PRINEVILLE/MITCHELL/JOHN DAY. Turn left (east) onto US 26. Travel 8.5 miles to a parking area signed RIMROCK SPRINGS WILDLIFE MANAGEMENT AREA, located on the left side of the highway. *DeLorme: Oregon Atlas & Gazetteer*: Page 51 A8.

The Hike

This short loop hike travels through a sagebrush-and-juniper landscape in the Rimrock Springs Natural Area. You'll start the hike by walking on a paved path for 0.6 mile to a side trail that leads to a wood viewing platform. From the platform you'll have nice views of a productive cattail marsh. Look for ducks, geese, and raptors. After enjoying the view, continue on the main trail as it climbs to the top of a small rise and travels next to some jumbled lava outcroppings. At 1.1 miles you can turn left and walk on a short side trail to a viewpoint of a wide valley and the Three Sisters Mountains in the background. You'll finish the loop at 1.4 miles and return to the trailhead on the paved path. After your hike, you can eat lunch at one of the picnic tables located at the trailhead.

Miles and Directions

0.0   Start walking on a paved path.

0.1   The trail forks. Go left to start the loop portion of the trail.

0.6 Arrive at a trail junction. (The paved path ends.) Turn left and walk on a side trail to a wood viewing platform. Go about 50 yards and arrive at the wood platform. Enjoy the views of the marsh, and then return to the main trail. Back at the main trail, turn left on the dirt path to continue the loop portion of the trail.

1.1 Arrive at a side trail that leads to a viewpoint on the left. Enjoy the views of the Three Sisters Mountains. After checking out the view, continue on the main dirt path.

1.4 The loop ends. Turn left onto the paved path.

1.7 Arrive back at the trailhead.

Madras

26 Tam-a-lau Trail at Cove Palisades State Park

This loop trail takes you more than 550 feet to the top of a high peninsula above Lake Billy Chinook in Cove Palisades State Park. From there you have far-reaching views of the vast reservoir below and the snowcapped Central Cascade peaks, including Mount Hood, Mount Jefferson, Broken Top, Mount Bachelor, and the Three Sisters. The Crooked, Deschutes, and Metolius Rivers feed this giant lake, which is popular with boaters.

Distance: 6.8-mile loop.
Approximate hiking time: 3½ to 4½ hours.
Elevation gain: 550 feet.
Trail surface: Paved path, steps, dirt path.
Best season: Open year round.
Other trail users: None.
Canine compatibility: Leashed dogs permitted.

Fees and permits: A $3 day use permit is required. You can purchase a day use permit at the park or purchase an annual Oregon State Parks permit for $25 by credit card by calling (800) 551-6949.
Schedule: Dawn to dusk.
Maps: Maptech CD: Coos Bay/ Eugene/Bend, OR.
USGS map: The Dalles, OR.

Finding the trailhead: From Redmond, travel 19 miles north on U.S. Highway 97 to a turnoff for Cove Palisades State Park and Culver/Round Butte Dam. Turn left (west) onto the Culver Highway and follow the state park signs for 6 miles to the park entrance. Follow the entrance road down into the canyon to a road junction. At the bottom of the canyon, turn left toward Deschutes Campground and day use areas. Continue 3.7 miles to another road junction. Turn left

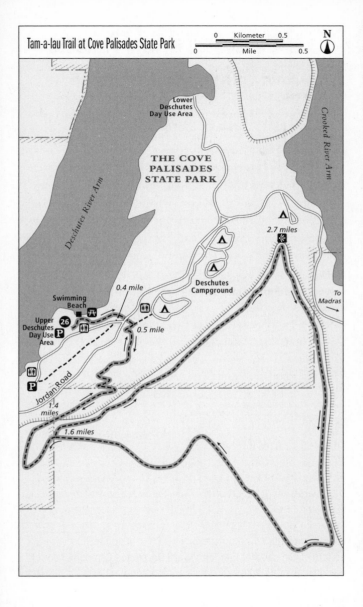

Tam-a-lau Trail at Cove Palisades State Park

THE COVE PALISADES STATE PARK

Lower Deschutes Day Use Area

Deschutes River Arm

Crooked River Arm

2.7 miles

To Madras

0.4 mile

Swimming Beach

Deschutes Campground

0.5 mile

Upper Deschutes Day Use Area

26

Jordan Road

1.4 miles

1.6 miles

Kilometer

Mile

N

toward the signed Deschutes Campground. Proceed 0.6 mile to a Tam-a-lau Trail sign. Turn right, go 0.3 mile, and turn right into the single car parking area.

If you are coming from Madras, follow US 97 north and then follow signs approximately 15 miles southwest to the park. Once you reach the park entrance, follow the directions described above. *DeLorme: Oregon Atlas & Gazetteer*: Page 57 D6.

The Hike

This high-desert hike gives you incredible views from a high rocky plateau called The Peninsula. The first 0.5 mile is a combination of paved paths and steps that take you into the campground. From the campground the route climbs at a steady pace for a little over a mile to the top of a long, flat plateau. The hillside is blanketed with bunch grass, yellow balsamroot, and purple lupine mixed with fragrant rabbitbrush and sagebrush.

After 1.6 miles you'll start the loop portion of the hike, located atop The Peninsula. This plateau is made up of rock and sediment that were deposited by the Deschutes River over thousands of years. The sediment and rock are mixed with layers of basalt, a result of massive lava flows that covered this area from different eruptions of Cascade volcanoes. The lava flows filled the three river canyons carved by the Deschutes, Metolius, and Crooked Rivers, water sources for Lake Billy Chinook. Over thousands of years, the rivers carved away the rock layers to produce the magnificent canyons that are present in this area today. After 2.7 miles you'll arrive at a dramatic viewpoint and a great place to take a break and eat lunch. After 5.2 miles you'll end the loop and descend on the same route back to your starting point. Avoid this hike during July and August, when temperatures can hover in the 90s. If you're visiting during those months, explore the trail in the cooler early morning—and be sure to bring plenty of water.

Miles and Directions

0.0   Begin by walking on the paved path at the northeast corner of the day use parking area. You'll travel a short distance and arrive at a grassy picnic area and swimming beach. From the picnic area, follow a paved path that heads uphill on the right side of the restrooms.

0.3   Turn right at the trail fork and continue, ascending a flight of steps.

0.4   Turn left at the trail fork and continue ascending the paved trail. Cross a paved road and walk through an opening in a fence around Deschutes Campground A.

0.5   Turn right onto a dirt path adjacent to a large interpretive sign. Over the next 1.1 miles, the trail ascends steeply to a high plateau above the lake.

1.4   Turn left onto a wide doubletrack road.

1.6   Turn left and begin the loop portion of the hike. Follow the dirt path as it parallels the edge of the rimrock and offers outstanding views of the lake canyon and the Central Cascade peaks.

2.7   Arrive at the tip of the peninsula, which serves as a good lunch spot.

5.2   The loop portion of the hike ends. Descend on the same route back to your starting point.

6.8   Arrive back at the parking area.

Prineville

27 Chimney Rock

This route takes you to the base of Chimney Rock—a prominent formation located high above the Crooked River. Along the way, you'll walk through a high-desert ecosystem of sage and juniper and enjoy views of the Crooked River Canyon and Cascade Mountains.

Distance: 2.6 miles out and back.

Approximate hiking time: 1 to 1½ hours.

Elevation gain: 500 feet.

Trail surface: Dirt path.

Best season: Open year round.

Other trail users: None.

Canine compatibility: Dogs permitted.

Fees and permits: No fees or permits required.

Schedule: Open all hours.

Maps: Maptech CD: Coos Bay/ Eugene/Bend, OR.

USGS map: Stearns Butte, OR.

Finding the trailhead: From U.S. Highway 26 in Prineville, turn south onto Main Street (Highway 27). Continue south for 17.1 miles to a gravel parking area on the left side of the road marked RIM TRAIL. The trailhead is located across from the Chimney Rock Recreation Area. *DeLorme: Oregon Atlas & Gazetteer:* Page 80 D1.

The Hike

If you're seeking solitude, you'll enjoy this hike that climbs to the base of Chimney Rock and provides nice views of Crooked River Canyon and the Central Cascade Mountains. From the trailhead you'll follow a series of switchbacks up a grass- and sage-covered hillside. With each step, the views of the river canyon become more dramatic.

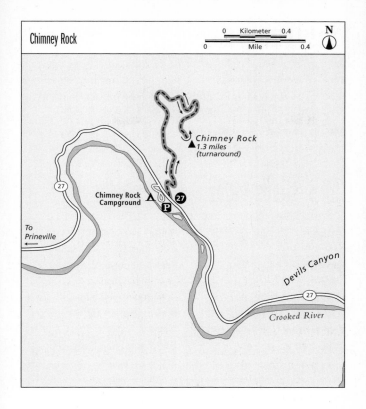

Chimney Rock
1.3 miles
(turnaround)

Chimney Rock
Campground

To
Prineville

Devils Canyon

Crooked River

As the trail climbs higher, you'll pass some twisted and gnarled juniper trees. Their stunted growth hides their age— some of the trees here are more than a century old. After 1.3 miles you'll arrive at the dramatic spire of Chimney Rock. Enjoy the views, and then retrace the same route back to the trailhead.

Miles and Directions

0.0 Start hiking on the marked dirt path.

1.0 Pass a rest bench.

1.3 Arrive at the base of Chimney Rock (your turnaround point). Retrace the same route back to the trailhead.

2.6 Arrive back at the trailhead.

28 Steins Pillar

Distance: 5.2 miles out and back.

Approximate hiking time: 2 to 3 hours.

Elevation gain: 700 feet.

Trail surface: Dirt path.

Best season: Open year round.

Other trail users: None.

Canine compatibility: Dogs permitted.

Fees and permits: No fees or permits required.

Schedule: Open all hours.

Maps: Maptech CD: Hermiston/ Prineville/Canyon City, OR.

USGS map: Salt Butte, OR; Steins Pillar, OR.

Finding the trailhead: Travel 9.1 miles east of Prineville on U.S. Highway 26. Turn left (north) onto Mill Creek Road (Forest Road 33). Travel 6.7 miles on Mill Creek Road (the road becomes gravel after 5.2 miles) to the junction with Forest Road 500. Turn right onto FR 500 and continue 2.1 miles to the trailhead on the left side of the road. *DeLorme: Oregon Atlas & Gazetteer:* Page 80 C2.

The Hike

Steins Pillar is a fascinating rock formation located in the heart of the Ochoco National Forest in the Ochoco Moun-

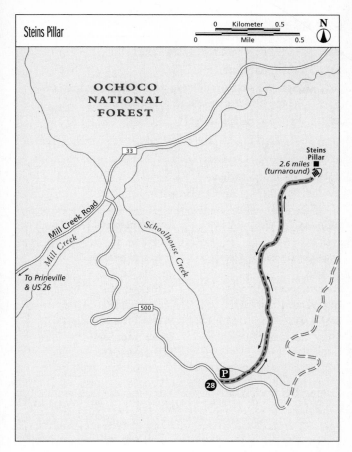

OCHOCO
NATIONAL
FOREST

33

Steins
Pillar
2.6 miles
(turnaround)

Mill Creek Road

Mill Creek

Schoolhouse Creek

To Prineville
& US 26

500

P

28

tains. The 350-foot pillar is an important geologic remnant of the area's rich volcanic history.

Nearly fifty million years ago, this was volcano land. Eruptions layered the area in volcanic tuff, andesite, and ash. The Clarno and John Day Formations, world famous for their many fossils, were created as a result of these eruptions. James Condon, a young Congregational minister and naturalist, first discovered fossils in the area in the 1860s. His first find was an ancient tortoise shell in Picture Gorge in the John Day Valley. Over the next several years, Condon and others uncovered many more plant and animal fossils—the precursor to research and cataloging of hundreds of specimens in the area over the next century. Fossils that have been discovered here include amynodonts and brontotheres of the Clarno Formation period (thirty-seven to fifty-four million years ago) and dogs, cats, camels, oreodonts, swine, rhinoceroses, and rodents of the John Day Formation period (twenty to thirty-nine million years ago).

A great way to get a feel for the geologic history of the area is by hiking the moderate 2.6-mile trail to the base of Steins Pillar. The trail starts out fairly flat through a dry, open forest of Douglas firs and then transitions into an open, rocky landscape filled with sagebrush and western juniper trees. The small, fragrant, bluish berries of the juniper are a favorite food of small birds and mammals. In spring and summer, wildflowers are scattered along the trail—bright red Indian paintbrush, bluish-purple lupine, and bright yellow mule's ears are just a few of the varieties you'll see.

After 1.2 miles the trail begins to descend the ridge, and the landscape shifts back to Douglas fir and ponderosa pine. Tree debris scattered on the forest floor along this section of trail appears to be the result of an old burn and frequent winter storms. Another mile up the trail, you'll catch your first glimpse of Steins Pillar as it rises prominently above the Mill Creek Valley and Steins Ranch. To reach the base of the pillar, descend a long series of steps for the remaining 0.3 mile. While at the pillar's base, look up to see why rock climbers find it such a tempting challenge. (The pillar was first climbed in 1950.) A 5.11A route heads up the northeast face, and a 5.10D climb shoots up the southeast face. These climbs are very difficult; some of the pitches are overhanging and cross sections of crumbly, rotten rock.

Miles and Directions

0.0 Start on the dirt track next to a Steins Pillar trail sign.

0.3 Begin climbing a ridge through a Douglas fir and ponderosa pine forest.

1.2 The trail starts descending.

2.3 Reach a viewpoint of Steins Pillar on your left.

2.4 Descend on a long series of wood steps.

2.6 Arrive at the base of 350-foot Steins Pillar (your turnaround point). Retrace the route back to the trailhead.

5.2 Arrive back at the trailhead.

29 Mill Creek Wilderness

You'll enjoy this beautiful and peaceful walk through the Mill Creek Wilderness, which includes abundant wildlife, wildflowers, and a meandering stream.

Distance: 5.4 miles out and back (with a longer option).
Approximate hiking time: 2 to 3 hours.
Elevation gain: 200 feet.
Trail surface: Dirt path and water crossings.
Best season: May through October.

Other trail users: Equestrians.
Canine compatibility: Dogs permitted.
Fees and permits: No fees or permits required.
Schedule: Open all hours.
Maps: Maptech CD: Hermiston/Prineville/Canyon City, OR.
USGS map: Steins Piillar, OR.

Finding the trailhead: From Prineville, drive 9.1 miles east on U.S. Highway 26 to Mill Creek Road (Forest Road 33). Turn left (north) and travel 10.6 miles to a fork in the road. Turn right at the WILDCAT CAMPGROUND sign. Drive 0.1 mile and turn right into a gravel parking area at the trailhead. Wildcat Campground is another 0.3 mile past the parking area. *DeLorme: Oregon Atlas & Gazetteer*: Page 80 B2.

The Hike

Located in the 17,000–acre Mill Creek Wilderness of the Ochoco National Forest, this route takes you on a trek along bubbling Mill Creek, passing through a forest of ponderosa pine, grand fir, and Douglas fir.

The trail begins with a series of creek crossings, so be sure to bring an old pair of tennis shoes or sandals to wear in the water. As you walk along the creek, you'll hear the cries

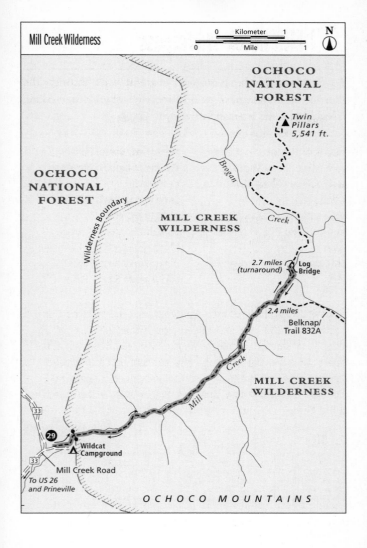

Mill Creek Wilderness

OCHOCO
NATIONAL
FOREST

▲ Twin
Pillars
5,541 ft.

Brogan

Creek

OCHOCO
NATIONAL
FOREST

Wilderness Boundary

MILL CREEK
WILDERNESS

2.7 miles
(turnaround)

Log
Bridge

2.4 miles

Belknap/
Trail 832A

Mill Creek

MILL CREEK
WILDERNESS

Wildcat
Campground

Mill Creek Road

To US 26
and Prineville

OCHOCO MOUNTAINS

N

0   Kilometer   1
0   Mile   1

of kingfishers protesting your presence on their home turf. Other birds in the area include pileated woodpeckers, wild turkeys, and northern goshawks. Pileated woodpeckers are the largest species of woodpecker and can be identified by their prominent red crests, black feathers, and white undersides. Northern goshawks, which weigh between six and eight pounds and live up to ten years, have slate-gray feathers and bright orange-red eyes outlined in white. You'll most likely see them weaving in and out of the woodlands with great speed and finesse as they hunt for small birds and mammals. If you don't first see a northern goshawk, you may hear its distinctive "ca-ca-ca" hunting cry. Other wildlife in this pristine wilderness area includes Rocky Mountain elk, mule deer, bobcats, cougars, and black bears.

As you continue on the trail, you'll pass green meadows of daisies, delicate purple aster, crimson penstemon, and bright purple thistle. Tall stocks of woolly mullein with their bright bunches of yellow flowers are also common. Shimmering green aspen trees grow in clusters along the banks of the creek, and cutthroat trout hang out in shady rock pools.

After 2.7 miles you'll arrive at your turnaround point at a log bridge. From here you have the option of climbing a series of long and winding switchbacks for 2.6 miles to the base of the 200-foot-tall Twin Pillars rock formation.

If you want to stay and explore this area more, pitch your tent at Wildcat Campground. The camping area is located just 0.3 mile northeast of the trailhead.

Miles and Directions

0.0   Start hiking on the signed Twin Pillars Trail #380.

0.1	Cross Mill Creek Road (Forest Road 33) and continue straight.
0.2	Proceed through a green metal gate and enter the Mill Creek Wilderness.
0.3	Wade across Mill Creek. After the creek the trail forks; turn left.
0.8	Cross the creek.
0.9	Cross the creek.
1.1	Navigate another stream crossing.
1.1	Cross the creek. Proceed approximately 100 yards and cross again.
1.5	Cross the creek.
2.1	The trail forks. Turn left and continue along the main trail.
2.2	Arrive at another stream crossing; logs are in place to help you cross. Walk another 50 yards and cross the stream again.
2.4	Cross the creek and arrive at a trail junction. Continue straight (left). (Note: Belknap Trail #832A goes right.)
2.5	Pass a sign on the left that reads TWIN PILLARS 2 MILES.
2.7	Arrive at a log bridge and your turnaround point. Retrace the same route back to the trailhead. (**Option:** You can continue another 2.6 miles up a steep ridge to the base of the Twin Pillars rock formation.)
5.4	Arrive back at the trailhead.

30 Painted Hills Unit–John Day Fossil Beds National Monument

The short hikes in the Painted Hills Unit of the John Day Fossil Beds National Monument provide a close-up look at the area's beautiful color-splashed hills and fascinating fossil beds. The Painted Hills Overlook Trail is a 1.0-mile out-and-back trail that takes you to the top of an overlook with views of the colorful surrounding hills. If you want more of an adventure, trek 1.5 miles to the top of Carroll Rim, where you'll have a sweeping view of the painted hills and surrounding high-desert country. If you want to see one of these hills up close, stroll the quarter-mile Painted Cove Trail. To view fossils of plants that dominated this area thirty-three million years ago, walk the Leaf Hill Trail. It's possible to complete all four of the established trails in just a day.

Distance:
A. *Carroll Rim Trail:* 1.5 miles out and back.
B. *Painted Hills Overlook Trail:* 1.0 mile out and back.
C. *Painted Cove Trail:* 0.25-mile loop.
D. *Leaf Hill Trail:* 0.25-mile loop.
Approximate hiking time: Varies depending on the trail(s) selected.

Elevation gain: Varies depending on the trail(s) selected.
Trail surface: Dirt path.
Best season: Open year round.
Other trail users: None.
Canine compatibility: Leashed dogs permitted.
Fees and permits: No fees or permits required.
Schedule: Open dawn to dusk.
Maps: Maptech CD: Hermiston/Prineville/Canyon City, OR.
USGS map: Painted Hills, OR.

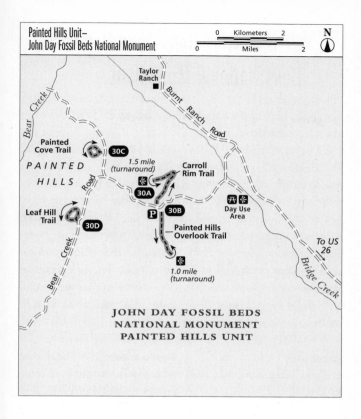

Kilometers 2

Miles 2

N

Taylor
Ranch

Burnt Ranch Road

Bear Creek

Painted
Cove Trail

30C

PAINTED
HILLS

1.5 mile
(turnaround)

Carroll
Rim Trail

30A

Road

30B

P

Day Use
Area

Leaf Hill
Trail

30D

Bear Creek

Painted Hills
Overlook Trail

To US
26

Bridge Creek

1.0 mile
(turnaround)

JOHN DAY FOSSIL BEDS
NATIONAL MONUMENT
PAINTED HILLS UNIT

Finding the trailhead: From Prineville, travel 45.2 miles east on
U.S. Highway 26 to the junction with Burnt Ranch Road, where a sign
indicates JOHN DAY FOSSIL BEDS NATIONAL MONUMENT—PAINTED HILLS UNIT. Turn left
(north) and go 5.7 miles. Turn left onto Bear Creek Road and proceed
0.9 mile to the turnoff for the Carroll Rim Trailhead. Turn left and then
take an immediate right into the gravel parking area on the right. The
Carroll Rim Trail begins on the opposite side of the road from the
parking area. Follow the road signs to reach the Painted Cove and
Leaf Hill Trails. *DeLorme: Oregon Atlas & Gazetteer*: Page 80 B3.

The Hike

The Painted Hills Unit of the John Day Fossil Beds National Monument has several hikes offering glimpses of the area's rich geologic history. The hikes are easy to moderately difficult, and each provides a different perspective on the area's unique formations.

The most striking feature you'll notice are the round, multihued hills of colorful claystone. Thirty million years ago, layers of ash were deposited in this area from volcanoes erupting to the west. Over millions of years, the forces of nature have carved and shaped the hills that you see today. Different elements such as aluminum, silicon, iron, magnesium, manganese, sodium, calcium, and titanium have combined to produce minerals that have unique properties and colors.

To get a bird's-eye view of the hills, take a short jaunt on the 1.0-mile out-and-back Painted Hills Overlook Trail, which takes you up a gentle ridge and includes several viewpoints along the way. If you want a close-up view of one of these unique painted hills, take a walk on the 0.25-mile Painted Cove Trail loop. A brochure and corresponding trail markers offer an in-depth look at these geologic formations. For instance, the colors of the hills change with the weather. When it rains, the clay absorbs water, causing more light reflection and changing the color of the hills from red to pink and from light brown to yellow-gold. As the hills dry out, the soil contracts, causing surface cracking that diffuses the light and deepens the color of the hills. The purple layer in the hill is the weathered remains of a rhyolite lava flow. Other colored bands in the hillside are due to differences in mineral content and weathering. Plants can't grow on the painted hills because the clay is so dense that moisture can't penetrate the surface. Also, the clay soil is nutritionally poor.

Another distinguishing landmark of the Painted Hills Unit is Carroll Rim, a high ridge consisting of John Day ignimbrite, better known as "welded tuff." More than twenty-eight million years ago, a volcano to the west erupted and hurled hot ash, debris, and gases into the air, which then landed and cooled to form a glasslike layer. To reach the top of this landmark and excellent views of the surrounding hills and valleys, hike the 1.5-mile out-and-back Carroll Rim Trail. From the top you'll be able to see Sutton Mountain, which rises prominently to the east.

For fossils, check out the 0.25-mile-long Leaf Hill Trail and its collection of ancient plants. The trail circles a small hill of loose shale deposits. While at first the hill seems somewhat unremarkable, a closer look reveals insights into the plants that once dominated here. The shales present in this hill were formed about thirty-three million years ago from lake-deposited volcanic ash. Fossils of thirty-five species of plants can be found at Laurel Hill, with alder, beech, maple, and the extinct hornbeam most prevalent. Other specimens include elm, rose, oak, grape, fern, redwood, and pine. Scientists have analyzed these plant fossils and concluded that this group of plants closely resembles two types of modern forests found in China—the mixed northern hardwood forest and the mixed mesophytic forest. Comparing the mix of plant species with these two modern forests indicates that in the past this area had a much higher rainfall content (up to 40 inches annually), milder temperatures, and a warmer climate than found here today. (Today the area receives about 12 to 15 inches of rain a year and experiences more extreme temperature variations.) In addition, the vegetation that grows here today is made up of high desert–type plants—juniper, sagebrush, and grasses.

Miles and Directions

A. *Carroll Rim Trail:* A 1.5-mile out-and-back trek to the top of Carroll Rim that offers sweeping views of the surrounding hills and valleys.

B. *Painted Hills Overlook Trail:* A 1.0-mile out-and-back path with a panoramic view of the Painted Hills.

C. *Painted Cove Trail:* This 0.25-mile loop circles a painted hill and gives you a close-up look at the unique properties of these interesting geologic formations.

D. *Leaf Hill Trail:* This 0.25-mile loop circles a hill where ancient plant fossils are abundant.

About the Author

Lizann Dunegan is a freelance writer and photographer who specializes in writing outdoor guidebooks and travel articles about the Northwest. Her other books include: *Canine Oregon, Best Easy Day Hikes Portland, Best Easy Day Hikes Oregon's North Coast, Hiking the Oregon Coast, Hiking Oregon, Mountain Biking Oregon: Northwest and Central Oregon, Road Biking Oregon, Trail Running Oregon,* and *Insiders' Guide to the Oregon Coast.* Lizann enjoys exploring the trails in Oregon with her partner, Ken Skeen; her dog, Bear; and her Andalusian horse, Miguel. Lizann also enjoys trail running, cycling, and spinning and knitting wool.